EYEWITNESS
DOG

Great Dane puppies

Bloodhound

Red fox

Skeleton of
maned wolf

Australian silky terrier

Shampooed
poodle

EYEWITNESS
DOG

Written by
JULIET CLUTTON-BROCK

Bronze Anubis,
c. 600 ce–300 bce

Australian terrier

English setter

Two Salukis

Arctic fox cub in
summer coat

Beagle
tracking

DK

Long-haired and miniature wire-haired dachshunds

Skull of fennec fox

Crossbred dog

LONDON, NEW YORK,
MELBOURNE, MUNICH, AND DELHI

Project editor Marion Dent
Art editor Jutta Kaiser-Atcherley
Senior editor Helen Parker
Senior art editor Julia Harris
Production Louise Barratt
Picture research Cynthia Hole
Special photography Jerry Young,
Alan Hills of the British Museum,
Colin Keates of the Natural History Museum

RELAUNCH EDITION (DK UK)
Editor Ashwin Khurana
US editor Margaret Parrish
Senior designers Rachael Grady, Spencer Holbrook
Managing editor Gareth Jones
Managing art editor Philip Letsu
Publisher Andrew Macintyre
Producer, preproduction Adam Stoneham
Senior producer Charlotte Cade
Jacket editor Maud Whatley
Jacket designer Laura Brim
Jacket design development manager Sophia MTT
Publishing director Jonathan Metcalf
Associate publishing director Liz Wheeler
Art director Phil Ormerod

RELAUNCH EDITION (DK INDIA)
Editor Surbhi Nayyar Kapoor
Art editors Deep Shikha Walia, Shreya Sadhan
Senior DTP designer Harish Aggarwal
DTP designers Anita Yadav, Pawan Kumar
Managing editor Alka Thakur Hazarika
Managing art editor Romi Chakraborty
CTS manager Balwant Singh
Jacket editorial manager Saloni Talwar
Jacket designers Govind Mittal, Suhita Dharamjit,
Vidit Vashisht

First American Edition, 1991
This American Edition, 2014
Published in the United States by DK Publishing
4th floor, 345 Hudson Street
New York, New York 10014

14 15 16 17 18 10 9 8 7 6 5 4 3 2 1
196448—07/14

A catalog record for this book is available from the Library of Congress.

ISBN 978-1-4654-2051-0 (Paperback)
ISBN 978-1-4654-2094-7 (ALB)

DK books are available at special discounts when purchased in
bulk for sales promotions, premiums, fund-raising, or educational use.
For details, contact: DK Publishing Special Markets, 345 Hudson Street,
New York, New York 10014 or SpecialSale@dk.com.

Color reproduction by Alta Image Ltd., UK
Printed by South China Printing Co. Ltd., China

Discover more at
www.dk.com

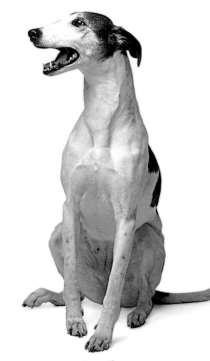

Raccoon dog in winter coat

Lurcher

Roman bronze, first century

Bronze dog from Egypt,
c. 300 BCE–300 CE

French bulldog

Contents

Boxer

What is a dog?

The dog family, called Canidae from the Latin *canis*, includes about 35 species of wolf, jackal, fox, and wild and domestic dog. Canids are carnivores (meat-eaters), with special adaptations for hunting: their teeth (p. 9) are used for killing, chewing, gnawing bones, and fighting; their senses of sight, sound, and smell (pp. 14–17) help them track prey; and most wild dogs have long legs for chasing prey. All canids are "digitigrade" (walk on their toes), with five claws on the front feet and four on the hind. Some domestic dogs have a fifth claw (dew claw) on the hind foot. Canids usually mate once a year and, after two months, produce a litter of pups (pp. 20–21). Like all mammals, the mother suckles her young and looks after them for several months.

Praying for prey
St. Hubert, patron saint of hunters, is shown with his hounds.

Distribution of dogs
Wild canids originally lived in every continent of the world, except Australasia, where they have been introduced by humans (pp. 36–37), and Antarctica.

North America
Europe
Asia
Africa
South America
Australia

Coat is multicolored and distinctive

Ears are small, erect, and rounded

The jovial jackal
There are three species of jackal (pp. 24–25)—the golden, the side-striped, and the black-backed. They all live in Africa; the golden jackal is also in Europe and Asia. Jackals live and hunt in pairs that stay together for life.

Golden jackal

Bushy tail, or brush

Red solitaire
The red fox is a solitary hunter of rabbits and rodents. The behavior of foxes (pp. 28–31) differs from other canids (pp. 18–19). All foxes have bushy tails.

Red fox

Doggy diversity

Dogs come in all shapes, sizes, and colors, with 400 breeds of domestic dog (pp. 48–61), all descended from the wolf, which was first tamed by humans about 12,000 years ago (pp. 8–9).

Warm feet

In the Middle Age, dogs were foot warmers for church congregations. In this stained glass (right) are the biblical characters Tobias and Sarah—and their dog.

Teeth usually number 42 (p. 9)

The largest canid

The wolf (pp. 22–23) is the largest wild canid and the ancestor of all domestic dogs (pp. 48–61). It lives and hunts in a pack and is the most social (pp. 18–19) carnivore.

Gray wolf

This wolf has thick gray fur, but the fur can vary from nearly pure white, red, or brown to black

African hunting dog

This social wild dog (pp. 18–19) hunts in family groups in the African grasslands (p. 26). It is in danger of extinction from disease, being killed by farmers, and losing prey to other predators.

African hunting dog

Muzzle is heavy and teeth are very different from a dog's

Shorter hind legs give typical crouching position

The striped hyena lives in Africa and western Asia. Hyenas are hunters and scavengers. Their powerful teeth crush bones

Long, powerful front legs

The Tasmanian wolf looked like a dog, but was a marsupial and unrelated to the dog family. It is now known only from stuffed specimens in museums

Rounded ears

Thick, muscular base of tail that did not wag

What is not a dog?

Hyenas, Tasmanian wolves (now extinct), and prairie dogs are not dogs. Hyenas (Hyaenidae family) are closer to cats. The Tasmanian wolf, or thylacine, was a marsupial (pouched mammal) in Australia. The North American prairie dog is a rodent related to squirrels.

Prairie dogs are social rodents that live in communal burrows of up to 160 acres (65 ha).

Dog family evolution

Thirty million years ago, during the Oligocene period, the first doglike creature, *Cynodictis*, appeared on the Earth. The earliest fossils of the dog family were found in North America. Another canidlike carnivore, *Tomarctus*, evolved during the Miocene period, from 24 million years ago. The genus *Canis*, which became *Canis lupus*, or wolf, then evolved some 300,000 years ago. From this wolf, the first domestic dogs date from about 12,000 years ago. The canids evolved into fast-running meat-eaters that hunted prey on open grasslands, as many of today's species do.

Be Sirius
The brightest star is Dog Star (Sirius) in the constellation *Canis Major*. Both space and dogs have evolved over millions of years.

Cranium (brain box)

Nasal bone

Upper jaw bone

Orbit for eye

Ear bone

Upper carnassial tooth for tearing flesh

Upper molar

Foramen magnum – entrance for the spinal cord to the brain

Cranium

Orbit

Palatal bone

Side view of *Cynodictis* skull

Palatal view of *Cynodictis* skull

Thirty-million-year-old head
This is the fossilized skull of one of the dog family ancestors—the mongooselike animal called *Cynodictis*.

Dire consequences
The extinct dire wolf (below) lived in California during the Ice Age. It was huge and preyed on the mammoth and other large Ice Age mammals.

Restoration of dire wolf

Dire wolves and a *Smilodon* attack a mammoth in California (right)

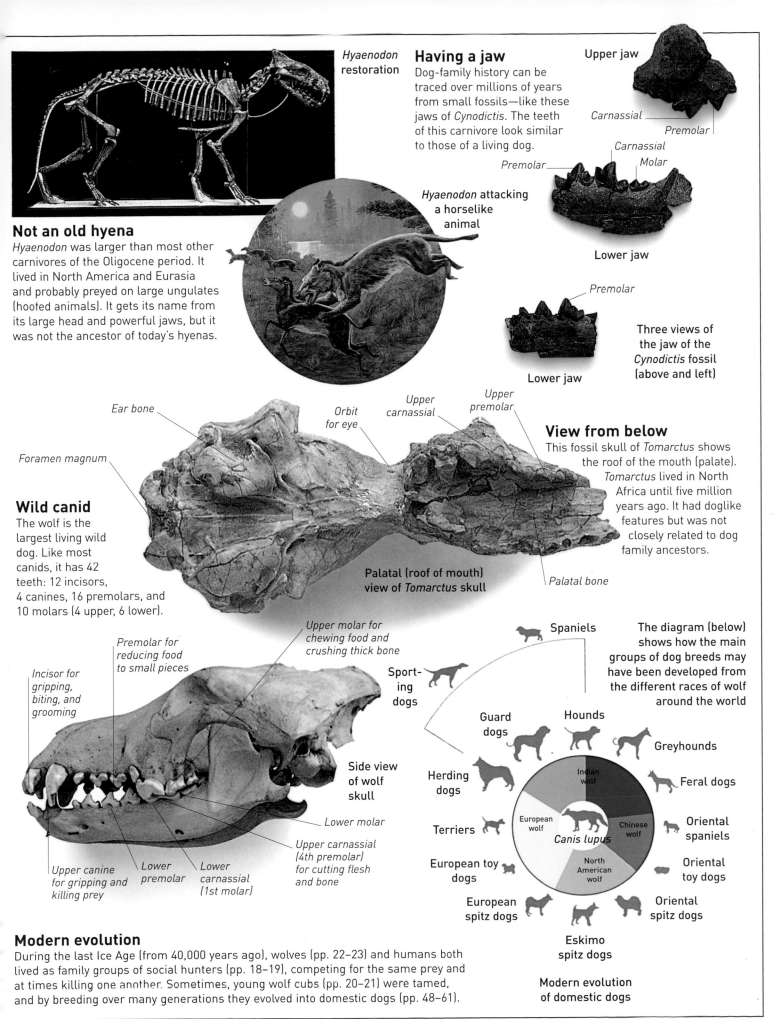

Hyaenodon restoration

Having a jaw
Dog-family history can be traced over millions of years from small fossils—like these jaws of _Cynodictis_. The teeth of this carnivore look similar to those of a living dog.

Upper jaw

Carnassial

Premolar

Carnassial

Molar

Premolar

Lower jaw

Not an old hyena
Hyaenodon was larger than most other carnivores of the Oligocene period. It lived in North America and Eurasia and probably preyed on large ungulates (hoofed animals). It gets its name from its large head and powerful jaws, but it was not the ancestor of today's hyenas.

Hyaenodon attacking a horselike animal

Premolar

Three views of the jaw of the _Cynodictis_ fossil (above and left)

Lower jaw

Ear bone

Orbit for eye

Upper carnassial

Upper premolar

View from below
This fossil skull of _Tomarctus_ shows the roof of the mouth (palate). _Tomarctus_ lived in North Africa until five million years ago. It had doglike features but was not closely related to dog family ancestors.

Foramen magnum

Wild canid
The wolf is the largest living wild dog. Like most canids, it has 42 teeth: 12 incisors, 4 canines, 16 premolars, and 10 molars (4 upper, 6 lower).

Palatal (roof of mouth) view of _Tomarctus_ skull

Palatal bone

Upper molar for chewing food and crushing thick bone

Premolar for reducing food to small pieces

Incisor for gripping, biting, and grooming

Side view of wolf skull

Lower molar

Upper canine for gripping and killing prey

Lower premolar

Lower carnassial (1st molar)

Upper carnassial (4th premolar) for cutting flesh and bone

Spaniels

Sporting dogs

Guard dogs

Hounds

Greyhounds

Feral dogs

Herding dogs

Oriental spaniels

Terriers

Oriental toy dogs

European toy dogs

European spitz dogs

Oriental spitz dogs

Eskimo spitz dogs

Indian wolf

European wolf

Canis lupus

Chinese wolf

North American wolf

The diagram (below) shows how the main groups of dog breeds may have been developed from the different races of wolf around the world

Modern evolution of domestic dogs

Modern evolution
During the last Ice Age (from 40,000 years ago), wolves (pp. 22–23) and humans both lived as family groups of social hunters (pp. 18–19), competing for the same prey and at times killing one another. Sometimes, young wolf cubs (pp. 20–21) were tamed, and by breeding over many generations they evolved into domestic dogs (pp. 48–61).

Dogs' bones

Mammal skeletons provide the body's framework, protecting and supporting key organs and allowing the body to move. Attached to the ends of the bones, elasticlike ligaments and tendons keep them joined yet moveable; muscles attached to bones enable the body to move in all directions. Each canid bone is characteristic of the dog family: the skulls of wolves, dogs, and foxes are long, with large teeth; the neck and backbone are long; the rib cage protects the chest; and the long limb bones are adapted for fast running.

Old mother hubbard
This nursery-rhyme old lady has no bones for her dog to chew (pp. 62–63).

Wolf skull can be recognized by the large size of the tearing, or carnassial, tooth

Large as life
Except for some domestic dogs, the wolf (pp. 22–23) has the largest dog family skeleton.

Arctic wolf

Neck vertebrae

Sternum

Elbow joint

Radius

Ulna

African hunting dog skeleton

African hunter
The African hunting dog (p. 26) has very long legs in relation to its body size, so is able to range over huge distances for prey.

African hunting dog

Red fox

Little red
The red fox creeps under bushes and rocks. It has shorter legs, compared to the size of its body, than the wolf.

Radius

Elbow joint

Ulna

Pelvis

Tibia

Ankle joint, or hock

Skeleton of red fox

Lower jaw

Shoulder joint

Sternum

Metacarpal bone

Skeleton of Maltese dog

Ball of fluff
This fluffy Maltese dog does not look like a wolf, but its skeleton is just like that of a tiny wolf.

Round skull

Neck is short, but still has seven vertebrae

Maltese dog

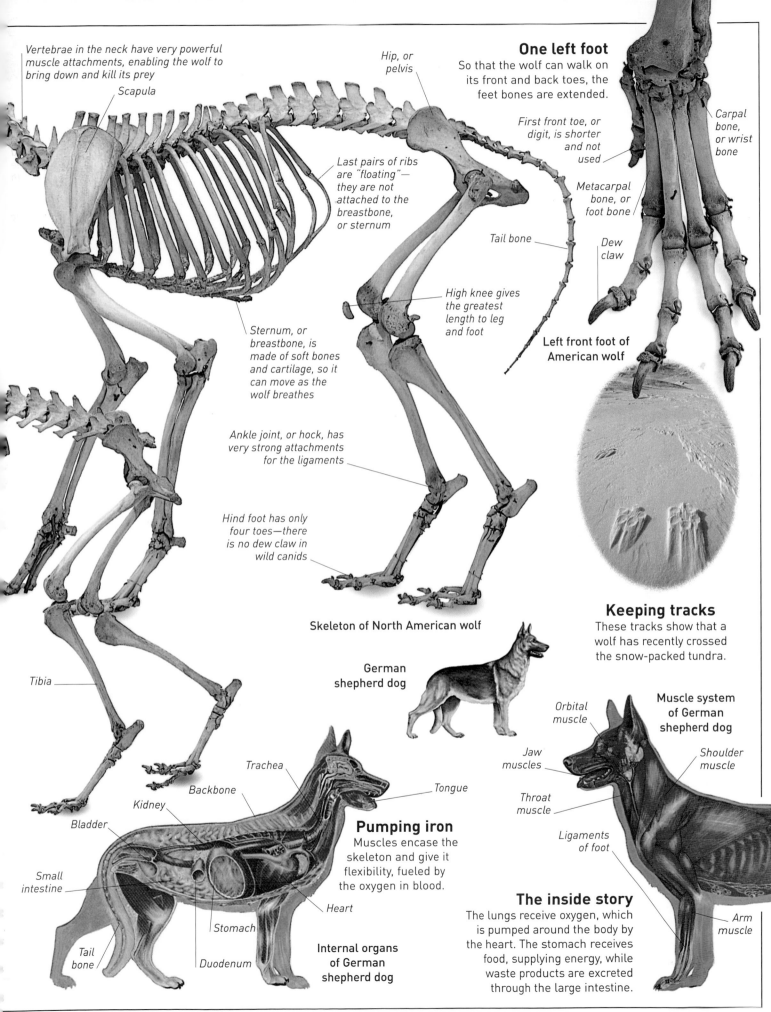

Vertebrae in the neck have very powerful muscle attachments, enabling the wolf to bring down and kill its prey

Scapula

Hip, or pelvis

One left foot
So that the wolf can walk on its front and back toes, the feet bones are extended.

First front toe, or digit, is shorter and not used

Carpal bone, or wrist bone

Last pairs of ribs are "floating"— they are not attached to the breastbone, or sternum

Metacarpal bone, or foot bone

Tail bone

Dew claw

Sternum, or breastbone, is made of soft bones and cartilage, so it can move as the wolf breathes

High knee gives the greatest length to leg and foot

Left front foot of American wolf

Ankle joint, or hock, has very strong attachments for the ligaments

Hind foot has only four toes—there is no dew claw in wild canids

Tibia

Skeleton of North American wolf

Keeping tracks
These tracks show that a wolf has recently crossed the snow-packed tundra.

German shepherd dog

Muscle system of German shepherd dog

Orbital muscle

Jaw muscles

Shoulder muscle

Throat muscle

Trachea

Backbone

Tongue

Kidney

Pumping iron
Muscles encase the skeleton and give it flexibility, fueled by the oxygen in blood.

Ligaments of foot

Bladder

Small intestine

Heart

The inside story
The lungs receive oxygen, which is pumped around the body by the heart. The stomach receives food, supplying energy, while waste products are excreted through the large intestine.

Arm muscle

Tail bone

Stomach

Duodenum

Internal organs of German shepherd dog

11

Coats, heads, tails

Fur keeps dogs warm: it is dense in cold climates, but short in hot ones. Fur is made up of two layers: a fine wool undercoat, usually of one color, and a top coat of longer, coarser hairs with natural oils to make it waterproof, and the striped (brindled) fur pattern. Colors are variations of white, black, and tan. All wild dog heads are long with erect ears, and teeth set in a line along straight jaws. Tails are all long, straight, often bushy, with a white or black tip, and used for balance, expressing feelings, and, when held up, as a signal to its group.

Fur coats
In the past, people needed clothing made from animal furs to keep warm. Today, with artificial materials available, wearing fur shows no regard for the dwindling numbers of wild animals, nor compassion for their suffering.

Many tails, like this Australian terrier's (p. 52), are docked so that the tail stands up straight

Red fox (pp. 28–29) tail is always reddish and bushy

Gray tree fox (pp. 28–29) has soft gray fur (left)

Sand fox (pp. 30–31) has fine, dense fur (above)

African hunting dog (p. 26) has short hair (above)

Thick tail of Bernese mountain dog (p. 56) keeps it warm

Dachshunds (p. 49) can be long-haired (right), short-haired, or wire-haired (far right)

Wire-hair of a miniature dachshund (above)

Dalmatian's (p. 55) tail even has spots on it

Hairy tail of giant schnauzer is cut short by docking (p. 55)

Losing their hair
Most dogs molt in spring and fall, so they have a thin coat in summer and a thick one in winter.

Side view of skull of Japanese Chin

Brain case (cranium)

Large orbit for cyc

Incisor tooth

Canine tooth

Lower jaw

A Japanese Chin
All dogs are descended from wolves, even Japanese Chins, (spaniels) with little, round heads and short, curved jaws.

Palatal (roof of mouth) view of Japanese Chin skull

Carnassial

Incisor

Hard palate

Ear bone

Zygomatic, or bony, arch at outside edge of eye socket

Dogs' ancestor
Wolves (pp. 22–23) have typical long heads.

Huge head

Canine tooth

Arctic wolf

Powerful nose

Bloodhound
This dog has a straight head, not a pronounced muzzle, and a powerful sense of smell for tracking (pp. 16–17).

Bloodhound

Bat-eared fox
This canid has smaller and four to eight more teeth than any other. Its head is still doglike.

Palatal view of bat-eared fox

Small molar for eating insects

Incisor

Hard palate

Straight profile to head

Fox terrier

Straight-laced
The fox terrier (p. 53) was bred to have a straight head.

Pekingese

Brain case (cranium)

Ear bone

Zygomatic, or bony, arch of eye socket

Nasal region

Incisor

Canine tooth

Lower jaw

Side view of skull of bat-eared fox

Flat face

Perky peke
Selective breeding (pp. 58–59) gave the Pekingese a round head, flat face, and floppy ears.

Sight, sound

Domestic dogs have inherited their eyes and ears from the wolf. All their senses have evolved for being a social hunter of large prey, and they have been developed in different breeds by "artificial selection." For example, in sight hounds (pp. 48–49), puppies with good sight were chosen as breeders, so, over time, the hounds developed even better sight. One change bred in most domestic dogs is that the eyes look forward (not to the side). Wolves and domestic dogs hunt at dusk, when sight is important. Foxes hunt at night, when hearing counts.

Hunting horn
Hunting dogs are trained to follow the sound of a horn and the human voice.

Dog's whistle
Most dogs will respond to the sound of a whistle.

Dense fur keeps the fennec warm on cold nights in the desert

Fennec fox
This smallest fox family member lives in the desert and is well adapted for keeping cool and finding food in the hot, dry sand.

Listening dog
The large, erect ears are turned each way as the dog figures out the direction of the sound.

Huge ears help the fennec keep cool and hear any sound—its next meal

The fennec's light-colored fur is pale to reflect the heat of the desert during the day

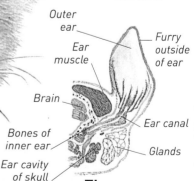

Outer ear
Ear muscle
Furry outside of ear
Brain
Ear canal
Bones of inner ear
Glands
Ear cavity of skull

The ear
All wild dogs have erect ears to help them tell where a sound has come from.

The belly fur is even paler, as it is on nearly every carnivore

Beautiful borzoi

The borzoi (pp. 46–47) is a sight, or "gaze," hound. With keen eyesight, it was used in the Middle East for game hunting, and later by Russian royalty in wolf hunts.

The eyes are large and face well forward so the borzoi probably has stereoscopic vision, which means that it can see in three dimensions like humans

Upper eyelid

Pupil

Iris

Lower eyelid

Third eyelid, or nictitating membrane

The eye

Dogs have a third eyelid, which protects the eye from dirt and dust.

Muzzles (p. 46) are usually worn by racing greyhounds

God of mummification

Anubis, a jackal-headed god in ancient Egypt, supervised embalming and weighed the dead's hearts.

When the upper teeth closely overlap the lower teeth, it is called a scissor bite

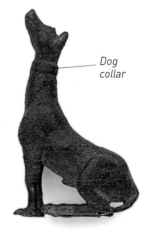

A winning greyhound

A greyhound's senses are directed forward at the start of a race. As it races, its eyes stay centered on the mechanical hare as though it were a live animal.

Maned wolf

The "maned wolf" (p. 33) of the South American savanna has very large ears for hearing in long grass.

Dog collar

The chase is on

This pack of African hunting dogs is chasing a gemsbok. They use their big eyes to see their prey, and their large ears to hear the communicating sounds of the pack and to hear if any other predators are trying to take over their prey.

Guard dog

This ancient Roman sculpture is watching and listening for any thieves at the door.

On the scent

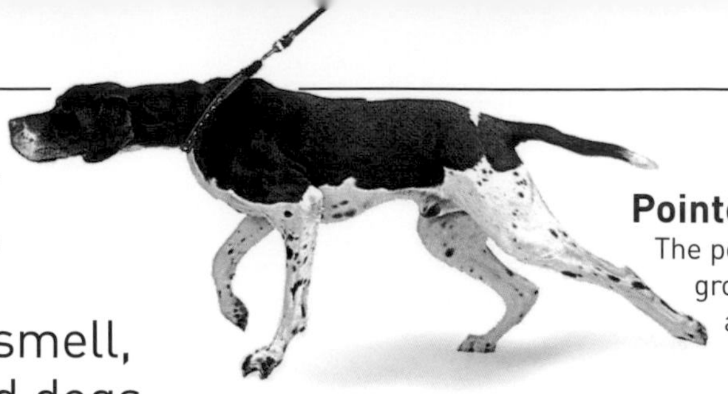

All canids have an acute sense of smell, and in all wild canids—wolves, wild dogs, jackals, and foxes—smell is the most highly developed sense. The animal hunts with its nose, finds its mate and identifies new beings in its territory with its nose, and can even tell if other animals are afraid by its smell. This is made possible by the long nose, which has rolls of thin bone that particles of scent are drawn over. With certain hunting dogs, there has been selection for the sense of smell. These dogs can smell very well, but are nearsighted.

Pointer pointing
The pointer ranges over the ground with its keen nose and then "points" out where the game is.

Who are you?
A dog can learn a lot by smelling the anal gland of another dog.

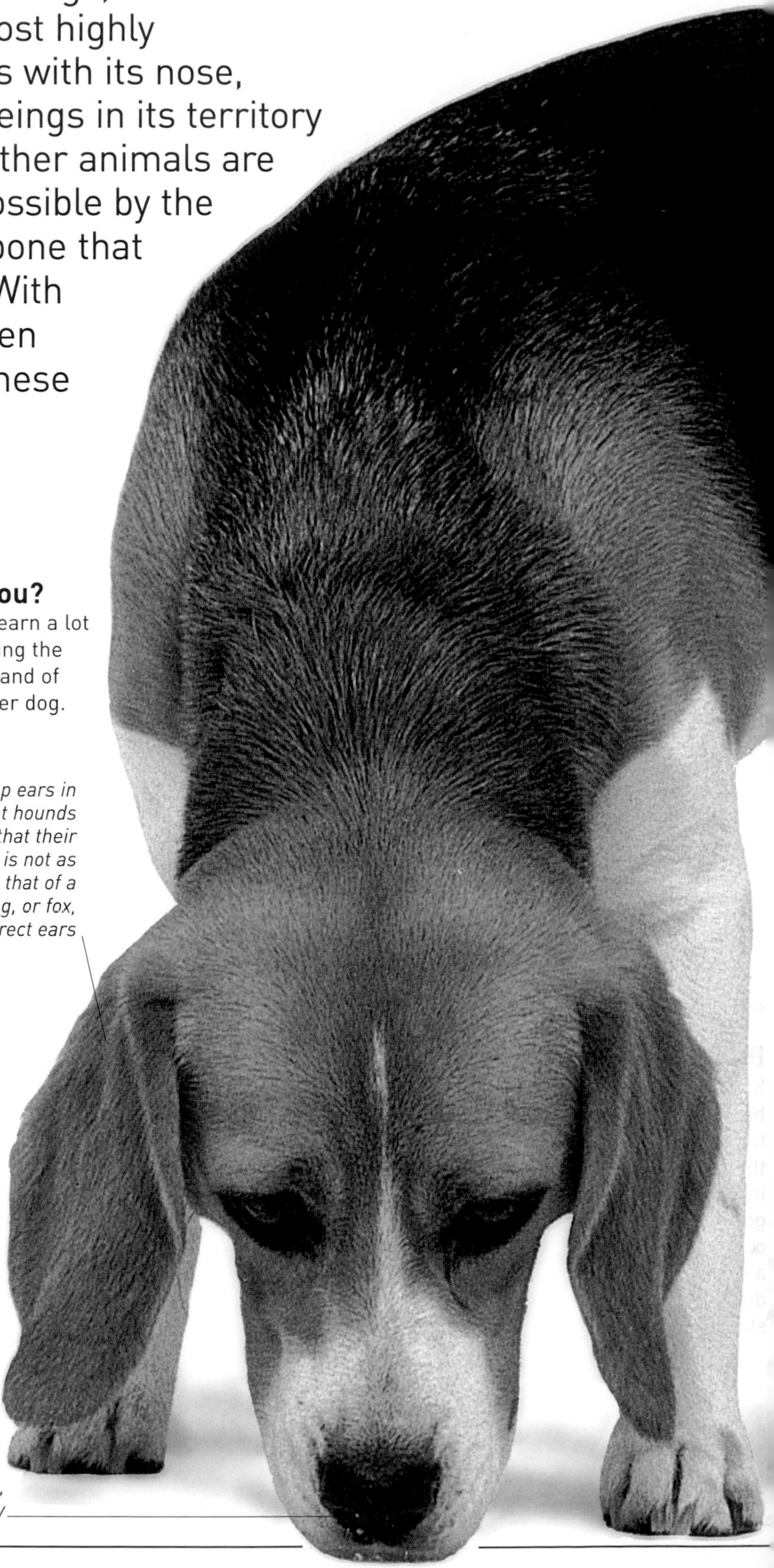

Drop ears in scent hounds mean that their hearing is not as good as that of a wild dog, or fox, with erect ears

Saluki

Dalmatian

Truffle hunting
Truffles grow underground and are a great food delicacy. In France, dogs are trained to search for truffles by their smell.

A nose, close to the ground, picks up any scents of prey

Attacking

Normally, a fox will not attack a full-grown sheep, but it might attack if it can smell that the sheep is already dying.

Nasal cavity

Nasal cavity with paper-thin turbinal bones

Cavity of brain

Sinuses

Fleshy nose

Lip

Palate

A dog's sense of smell is due to rolls of fine bone (turbinals) in its nasal cavity. These are connected to nerves that send messages to the brain.

Mini dachshund's nose

All the dog family have leathery noses and two nostrils, which draw scents into the nasal cavity.

The bat-eared fox's keen sense of smell allows it to find its prey quickly

Bat-eared fox

This fox eats any small animal or fruit that it can find. It needs a good sense of smell to find beetles underground.

Strong legs and stamina make a dependable hunter

Beagle

Scent hounds, like this beagle, have been bred to use their noses more than their eyes and ears in the hunt. With less good hearing, the dog can concentrate on tracking a scent without being distracted by slight noises.

Looking for prey...

... and finding a surprise

English setter

These scent hounds "set up" birds from the ground for shooting in the air.

Behavior

Behavior in the dog family is divided into two groups. Solitary hunters—foxes and South American wild dogs (pp. 28–33)—live on their own, except when mating and rearing young; social hunters—wolves, jackals, coyotes, African hunting dogs, dholes (pp. 22–27), and domestic dogs (pp. 14–17)—behave like a human family, where parents lead and children do as they are told until they are old enough to leave. In a wolf pack, every wolf knows which dogs are above or below it in the family hierarchy and will fight hard to keep or better its position.

Ears back show dog is afraid—or even potentially aggressive

Dog appears happy and relaxed—with pert ears and smiling mouth

Crossbred dog

Getting to know you
The strong, dominant wolf on the left greets the weaker, more submissive wolf.

Ears laid back show fear or aggression

Tail between legs shows a submissive stance

Mouth shut tightly denotes apprehension

German shepherd dog

Body language
Dogs can say all they need to each other by the postures of their bodies and tails.

Just good friends
This painting by English artist John Charlton shows dogs of indistinct breeds (pp. 60–61) exhibiting their friendliness with one another.

Crouched body means fox is waiting to pounce

Alert ears show fox is listening out for prey

Solitary hunters

Foxes, such as this American gray fox (pp. 28–29), are solitary hunters that hunt by themselves, and so do not have the interactive behavior of social hunters. A fox's tail cannot wag as expressively as a wolf's, and its ears are not so mobile. Even so, a fox will cower down to make itself look small if frightened and will stand up tall to look threatening if angry.

Gray tree fox

Two wolves fighting it out to see which one will be the leader

Social hunters

The African hunting dog and other social hunters must provide meat for the family group and defend themselves against other large predators. Human hunters are their main competitors. The wolf (pp. 22–23) has been wiped out in much of Europe and Asia; the African hunting dog and the dhole (pp. 26–27) are also close to extinction.

Howlin' wolves
Like its wolf ancestors, this pointer howls if on its own to communicate with others of its kind. Some dogs howl when they hear music.

Top dog
Although smaller than the Dalmatian, this Norfolk terrier has the stronger personality and is showing that he is top dog.

Dalmatian's head is slightly turned away, showing fear

Norfolk terrier's positive stance shows his confidence toward the larger dog

Dalmatian

Norfolk terrier

Fighting
At a kill, African hunting dogs eat extra meat that is regurgitated for their young or other pack members, who will fight over the half-digested morsels.

Pointer

Dogs' club
This caricature by J. J. Granville emphasizes the similarity of dog behavior with that of humans.

Puppies

The young of the dog family (Canidae) all look similar when newborn—small, defenseless, blind, short-haired with short legs and a little tail, and eat by sucking milk from their mother. The number of young can vary from one to 12 or more. After several days, their eyes open, they begin to hear, and they need solid food. This is provided by the mother and, in social species, by other group members, who regurgitate meat they have eaten. In the wild, young are born in a den (hole in the ground); a domestic dog also needs a dark, warm place to give birth 63 days after mating.

Foxy food
This mother fox has a rabbit for her cubs who are waiting in their den.

Four-week-old Great Dane puppies...

... playfully attacking each other...

It's playtime
All puppies should be allowed space to play. They need exercise to grow properly, but they also need to learn social interaction with other dogs and humans. Here, two puppies are learning to relate to one another.

... with one trying to dominate the other

All is well—they're friends again

Looking endearing
Great Dane puppies (above and left) have the same needs as a Pekingese or wolf. But these giant dogs require lots of wholesome meat, extra calcium, vitamins, and large bones to chew (pp. 62–63). They also need space to exercise their growing limbs.

Six-week-old Great Dane puppies

Nursing
This wolf is suckling her cubs. Soon, their sharp milk teeth will grow and hurt her nipples, so she will wean the cubs with regurgitated meat.

Learning to behave
The play of these African hunting dog pups teaches them social behavior rules, setting them up for adult life as powerful hunters.

A small bronze Greek sculpture of a pregnant female—from the fifth century CE

Four-and-a-half-month-old black Labrador puppy

Dalmatian at six months

A tail of two puppies
This Dalmatian is older than the black Labrador and is the dominant dog. Both are half-grown; in a few months they could be fighting in earnest.

Getting carried away
Canids carry their cubs by the scruff of the neck. Usually it is the mother who carries pups, but sometimes the father does.

Wolf-boys
Legend says Rome was founded by Romulus and Remus, who were suckled as babies by a she-wolf.

Pack leader

Wolf packs are like human families—the oldest male and female are leaders, and the young do as they are told. Wolves and humans have many social-behavior patterns in common, for both evolved as social hunters working as a team to kill larger animals. Wolves guard their territory and make their presence known by howling (p. 19). Each pack member knows his or her position in the dominance scale. The only wolves to mate are the dominant male and female. After birth, the father brings meat for the mother. The cubs are suckled for about 10 weeks, then fed with regurgitated meat until they start hunting with the pack. As the cubs grow older, they learn to keep their place in the pack.

Follow the leader
This group of European wolves follows its leader to look for prey and will eat anything it finds, even insects and berries. Wolves range over 400 sq miles (1,000 sq km) in packs of up to 20.

Erect ears show it is on the alert— for prey or foe

European gray wolf
Wolves have been slaughtered by humans for hundreds of years. European wolves are now found only in some parts of Europe.

Sharp teeth enable wolf to kill its prey quickly

Multicolored
Arctic wolves have a hard time finding prey in the freezing Arctic Circle. They have a thick, white winter coat to camouflage them in snow and ice, but can be shades of gray, buff, or black during summer. They have short tails and small ears to keep the body as compact as possible. Arctic wolves feed on hares, birds, and, if they are lucky, deer or musk ox.

Little Red Riding Hood
This story of a very clever wolf tricking a girl frightened children from going into forests alone.

A rare red wolf
Smaller than the gray wolf and adapted for the warm southeastern US, red wolves were extinct in the wild until their reintroduction in 1988.

Win or lose
Wolves are quick to snarl and they fight often, but a wolf will seldom be killed in a fight. It can be badly hurt, though.

Trouble ahead for brave novice
According to Nootka Indian legend, from northwest US, novices were sometimes carried away by wolves. This club, made of abalone shell, bone, and human hair, may represent the powers the brave received during captivity.

Ethiopian howler
The Ethiopian wolf is in danger of extinction because the high grassland plains where it lives are being taken over by farmers for livestock grazing. There may be only 500 of these tawny-red wolves left in the wild.

Long, powerful legs allow the wolf to range over huge distances for prey

Making a meal of it
A pack of wolves chase musk oxen on Ellesmere Island, Canada.

The tail of this wolf is pointing down, showing it is wary of what is ahead

Jackals

Wolves are some of the most social hunters on land; jackals and coyotes come just below them in the scale of social hunters (pp. 18–19). There are three species of jackal, all found in Africa: the side-striped jackal and the black-backed jackal are found south of the Sahara; the golden jackal is the most widespread, and is also found in southeastern Europe and southern Asia. Coyotes are found only in North America. Jackals and coyotes live in close-knit family groups that forage for food, either scavenging kill left by other carnivores or killing something themselves. The whole family helps to look after pups and bring back food.

Limestone stele of ancient Egyptian kneeling before the jackal of Wepwawet, with 63 other jackals

A fierce face
Mexican Toltecs worshiped a serper god, Quetzalcoatl, shown here with a 7th–9th century coyote headdress of shell and wood

Golden oldies
This pair of golden jackals will stay together for life, hunting and breeding together and patrolling their territory together, scent-marking it with urine to prevent other jackals from coming near.

Silver saddle
The black-backed jackal has a coat of fine fur with a black, or silver, saddle.

This mummified canid in the form of the jackal god, Anubis, is from ancient Egypt, 600 BCE–300 CE

Social coyote

The coyote is also called brush, or prairie wolf, and is the jackal of North America—a social hunter (pp. 18–19) that lives in pairs and family groups.

Canid

This golden jackal is doing a quick turn in its lookout for prey.

Cunning coydog

Wild coyotes may mate with domestic dogs. Their "coydog" pups are not wild or tame, and may kill domestic livestock for food.

Skull is smaller than a wolf's, with a flat forehead and small teeth

Dog dance

Dogs were highly regarded by Native Americans, for meat and transportation (pp. 56–57). This painting by Swiss artist Karl Bodmer shows a medicine man of the Missouri-River-dwelling Hidatsa tribe in a special costume performing a "dog dance."

Coarse, short-haired coat varies from gold to brown, depending on season and region

White stripe

The side-striped jackal's coat is a mix of gray, tawny, white, and black. A white stripe runs along its side; it has a white-tipped tail.

Jackal worship

Anubis, the jackal god, is frequently shown in ancient Egyptian artifacts.

African–Asian dogs

Cape fox
The most southern of the true foxes, South Africa's Cape fox is a small, solitary hunter with a silvery coat that lives in dry places and hunts at dusk.

Many wild dogs live in Africa and Asia and are social hunters. Jackals (pp. 24–25) live on both continents, and wolves (pp. 22–23) live in Asia. In Africa, there are hunting dogs (pp. 6–7) and bat-eared foxes (p. 13, p. 17), which are not actually foxes. In India and Southeast Asia, there are "red dogs" (dholes) and raccoon dogs, which are also found in Japan. True foxes (pp. 28–29) that are solitary hunters (pp. 18–19) are the Tibetan and Bengal foxes. Each wild dog or fox has evolved to fill a particular role in its environment's hierarchy, interacting with both prey and other predators.

Large, rounded ears

Short, broad face and muzzle

Thin but muscular legs

A most sociable dog
The African hunting dog is one of the most social dog family members. It is not a dog; it belongs to the genus *Lycaon*. It lives in a large pack on grasslands with an elaborate communication system of sounds and movements. The pack ranges over a huge area to hunt by day, and is vulnerable to disease, parasites, other hungry carnivores, and humans.

Unique coat pattern is tan and gray with large, white blotches

White tuft at the end of the short, bushy tail acts as a flag

African hunting dog

Having no dew claw on the front foot makes the hunting dog unique

Bat-eared fox

Very large ears, up to 5 in (12 cm) long

Dark gray to black on face mask and muzzle

Very long tail—up to 13 in (34 cm) in length

Enough teeth
The bat-eared fox (p. 17) has 46–50 teeth (other canids have 42) and feeds mostly on insects.

Two-headed charm
This dog-headed medicine figure from Bakongo in the Democratic Republic of Congo, Africa, is used by driving nails into its wooden body to activate the forces within.

Indian or Chinese?

The red dog, or dhole, is a social hunter (pp. 18–19) and will not interbreed with domestic dogs. The Chinese dhole has a thicker, darker coat than the more southern Indian dhole.

Rounded ears

Tawny-colored coat

Long, bushy tail

Dark red coat

Chinese dhole

Indian dhole

Tail darker color than rest of coat

On top of the world

The Tibetan fox has a thick coat for life on Tibet's high, cold plateaus. It has long slender jaws for pulling rodents out of their burrows.

Tail is short, relative to its body length

White variety of coat shows this dog has been bred in captivity for its fur

Short, sharply pointed muzzle

Raccoon dog in winter coat

When is a raccoon not a raccoon?

The raccoon dog is a chubby canid with a short tail and a thick, fine coat of gray-black and white fur highly valued by the fur trade (p. 13), and so widely bred in captivity. In the USSR, captive animals were allowed to go wild, and they now live as feral populations (pp. 36–37).

Short, erect ears rounded at top

Bengal fox

This small, red fox lives on open grasslands and scrub in India and digs its own dens. It hunts rodents, lizards, and other small animals.

Black facial mask, like that of a true raccoon

Raccoon dog in dark summer coat

True raccoons are Procyonidae

Red or gray?

The quack frog
Aesop's fable tells of a frog who said he was a doctor. The fox asked why he did he not heal his own walk and wrinkled skin.

All foxes are solitary hunters that live on their own (pp. 18–19)—except in mating season. They have long bodies, bushy tails (a "brush"), highly developed senses (pp. 14–17), and large, erect ears. Their usual prey are rodents and rabbits. The red fox is very common, known for its cunning and for being able to adapt to different environments—deserts, mountains, and cities. There are 10 other species in the fox group, or genus *Vulpes* (pp. 26–27, 30–31). The gray fox of North and Central America belongs to the genus *Urocyon* and can climb trees.

Waiting for lunch
Fox cubs (pp. 20–21) stay with their mother for months before they find their own territories.

Making tracks
Fox paw prints are smaller than those of most dogs—the pad marks are longer, and the claws are sharply pointed.

Coat can range in color from grayish and rust-red to a flame red

Furry beautiful
The red fox's fur is so beautiful that people have made clothes from their pelts for thousands of years. Captive foxes have also been bred for their furs. Today, clothes made of animal furs are unacceptable to many people (p. 12).

The tail of the red fox, which has a white tip, does not express the fox's feelings the way a dog's tail does

Getting to the top

The gray tree fox is found in the US, Central America, and northern South America. It is gray like salt and pepper and has reddish underparts.

A gray tree-climbing fox on the lookout for prey, which can be rabbits, insects, or dead animals (carrion)

Tip of the tail may be blackish, or gray like the coat

Nose and sides of muzzle are black

A bird in view

The red fox does not climb trees, but the gray fox spends much of its time in trees, searching for birds and eggs to eat.

Fox's acute sense of smell enables it to cover up to 6 miles (10 km) in search of food

Throat and chin have light, or white-colored, fur

A hunting we will go

In many countries, fox hunting is a country sport. Foxes are successful carnivores and can become pests by killing chickens and game birds. Hunting controls fox numbers, but many people think it is cruel.

Streetwise

In some cities, foxes are common. They kill rats, scavenge in trash cans, and learn road sense.

Deep in the forest

English artist William Morris had a great regard for the natural world. To him, the fox was an essential part of every woodland scene.

Black or red?

American artist John James Audubon painted a variety of wildlife, including the black, or melanistic, form of the red fox.

Hot and cold foxes

A few foxes live harsh lives in the coldest and hottest climates. The Arctic fox lives in the icy regions of northern Europe, Asia, Alaska, and Canada. It has short ears to stop heat loss, dense fur to keep warm, and it can cover up to 15,000 acres (6,000 hectares) in search of food. Other fox species live in hot deserts where there is little food, and they hunt and scavenge across huge areas. The foxes that live in hot, dry deserts all have very large ears to stay cool, small bodies that need little food, and short, dense fur. They sleep in dens during the daytime heat, and then hunt by night when it can be very cold.

Desert fox
The fennec fox is the smallest fox. It lives in the parched deserts of Arabia and Africa's Sahara, where there are few other animals and so food is always scarce.

Soft, dense coat is designed to keep the Arctic fox warm, and is thicker in winter

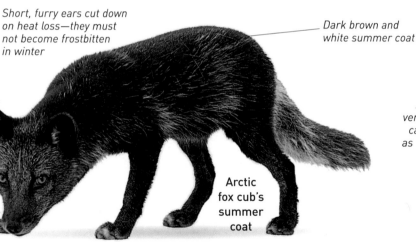

Short, furry ears cut down on heat loss—they must not become frostbitten in winter

Dark brown and white summer coat

Arctic fox cub's summer coat

Adult's tail is very bushy, and can be as long as 12 in (30 cm)

Coat of many colors
An Arctic fox with a white, or polar, winter coat (right) lives in the high Arctic, where there is usually snow. In summer, this fox will have a brown-and-white coat (above). A less common variety of Arctic fox, the "blue" fox has a steely-gray winter coat, but in summer is brown all over. Molting occurs in spring and fall, when it is time for a color change.

A pair of Arctic foxes—one in a dark summer coat, the other in a pale winter coat

Hind foot has a thick covering of soft fur all over it—and under the pads

Big ears of the sand fox are typical of "hot foxes," but not quite so big as those of the fennec

Half a fennec fox, half a red fox

This small desert fox from North Africa and the Arabian Desert looks like a fennec fox, with its small body and big ears, but its skull, teeth, and coloring are similar to the red fox's (pp. 28–29).

A whiter shade of pale

The pale fox lives in grasslands at the southern edge of the Sahara Desert in Africa. Like the fennec, it is a small, pale-colored fox.

Long, bushy tail can be curled around the body to keep it warm during cold desert nights

Rüppell's sand fox

After a meal

The fennec needs sharp senses (pp. 14–15) and quick movements to catch jumping rodents.

Thick ruff of very fine fur around the neck

Swiftly, swiftly

The kit, or swift, fox is the only desert fox in North America. Today, it is only in southwestern US and Mexico; many were poisoned by bait meant for coyotes.

The kit fox lives in the deserts of North America

Adult Arctic fox in pale winter coat

Thick fur on feet almost hides claws

31

Foxy zorro

South American wild dogs are often called foxes, or *zorros* (Spanish for foxes), but are not true foxes (pp. 28–29). They are solitary hunters (pp. 18–19) of small animals, but will eat anything they find. There are three groups, or genera, of foxlike dogs: the short-legged bush dog, maned wolf, and seven members of the *Dusicyon* genus, like the crab-eating *zorro* that is sometimes tamed by the Indians to go hunting with them. Another fox, named "Falkland Island wolf" by English naturalist Charles Darwin, was killed off by fur traders in the late 1800s.

Culpeo's coat
This *Dusicyon* member has a grayish-yellow and black coat, which is not in demand, so the fox is not endangered.

Stirrup vessel—with a fox on a man's forehead—from Mochica tribe of pre-Columbian Peru, 300–1000 CE

Pretty Patagonian
The Patagonian fox, or chilla, lives in the southern part of South America. Like many canids in the genus *Dusicyon*, it is not at all timid.

Red and gray
Found in the pampas, this gray-bodied, red-headed *zorro* has a very long, bushy tail.

Azara's *zorro*

Small ears

Broad face

Bush dog

Reddish-tan, or tawny, coat

Very short legs

Bush dog
Like other South American members of the dog family, the bush dog is not a true dog or fox, but belongs in a group—the genus *Speothos*—on its own. Looking more like an otter or badger, it is found in open country near water in tropical South America. It spends much of its time in a burrow.

Large, erect ears with white fur inside

Dark muzzle

Erect mane with darker fur running down nape of neck and back

Little ears
The small-eared dog, or *zorro*, is rare. It lives in tropical rain forests, but nothing is known of its habits.

Magnificent mane
The maned wolf—in the genus *Chrysocyon*—is different from other dog-family members as its tail is short and its legs are longer than its body. It is not a wolf or a fox, but is called the "stilt-legged fox." It lives in southern Brazil's tall grass and woods and pounces on small animals.

Maned wolf

Maned wolf with its short, bushy tail

Nazca pottery fox from coast of Peru, 500 BCE–600 CE

Very long, stiltlike legs

Reddish-yellow coat

The crab-eating zorro
This brindled-gray fox probably does not often eat crabs, living in the tropical forests of northeastern South America.

Dark-colored fur on legs and feet make it look as if it is wearing stockings

Domestication

Egyptian papyrus, c. 1500–1200 BCE, showing two jackals and some goats

The wolf is the ancestor of all domestic dogs (pp. 48–61). Some breeds may look very different from the wolf and each other, but every dog feels and behaves like a wolf. Humans probably first tamed wolves during the last Ice Age. The people of Ancient Egypt and western Asia were the first to breed distinctive kinds of dogs. By Roman times, most of the different shapes and sizes of dogs that we know today already existed. This is known from skeletal remains, but also from works of art that portray the animals in detail. In the ancient world, dogs were kept as hunting, herding, and guard dogs (pp. 40–45), for sport (pp. 46–47), and companionship.

Jackal god
The jackal has always been linked with humans, but it is not an ancestor of the domestic dog. Anubis (left), a jackal god, was an ancient Egyptian deity.

Handle decorated with coral

Persian plaque
This stylized half-dog, half-bird—or "fenmurv"—is a fertility symbol. Made of silver during the Sassanian dynasty (c. seventh century BCE) this object was found in India.

Flagon
This Celtic bronze drinking vessel (c. 400 BCE) shows two hounds chasing a duck, which seems to be swimming when liquid is poured.

Huntsmen
Assyrian huntsmen with mastifflike hounds walk in a royal park. This bas-relief is from Ashurbanipal's Palace at Nineveh (built 645–635 BCE).

Eastern worship

In the Far East, dogs have many purposes and are included in religious worship. This stone temple god, in the form of a lionlike dog, is from Thailand.

Greek urn

This vase is of Greek design (c. 380–360 BCE), although it was found in southern Italy. The girl is dangling a tortoise to tease her pet dog. The bracelets on her ankle ward off evil spirits.

Townley hounds sculpture was found at Monte Cagnolo, Italy, in the late 1700s

Townley hounds

The ancient Romans kept dogs. They used greyhounds and bloodhounds for hunting, and large mastiffs as fighting and war dogs.

Woman and dog

This is the skeleton of a woman, buried with her hand resting on her dog. The skeletons were found in Israel and date back to about 12,000 years ago. This is one of the earliest examples of a domestic dog ever discovered.

Cave canem

Just as today "Beware of the dog" is written on gates, the Romans wrote *Cave canem*, which means the same in Latin.

Dogs' collars

Ever since Egyptian times, dogs in paintings and sculpture have been shown wearing collars.

Italian brass collar

German spiked iron collar

Silver presentation collar

Dog rose

The ancient Greeks used this flower to treat people bitten by rabid dogs.

Pottery vessel—from the Colima, Mexico, 300–900 CE—of a hairless, fattened "techichi" dog

Feral dogs

The first dogs, descended from wolves, were domesticated about 12,000 years ago. Some reverted to life in the wild (although they would still scavenge scraps from human hunters) and are known as "feral" dogs. In some places, dogs live and breed without any human contact at all. The most successful of all feral dogs is the dingo of Australia. There are also feral, or pariah (meaning outcast), dogs in Asia, and in Africa where they live on the outskirts of villages and clean up the garbage; there is often not enough food for the people, let alone the animals, so the dogs must fend for themselves.

Ferreting for food
The feral dogs of Egypt are sometimes lucky and find scraps of food left by tourists.

In the wilds of India
Pariah dogs have been living wild in India for thousands of years. Some look very like the dingoes of Australia.

Santo Domingo dog
This dog is probably similar to the wild dogs that Christopher Columbus found in the West Indies.

Peruvian pariah
The native peoples of South America, had dogs, which lived around their settlements, just like the feral dogs of today.

Quinkan spirits
In these cave paintings near Cape York in Australia, the "Quinkan spirits" (Aborigines' Great Ancestors) are escorted by a dingo.

Nose is used for scenting prey—lizards, rabbits, or rodents—but sometimes fruit or plants

A sitting dingo

Eye of a dingo is more like that of a wolf than a dog

Dominant dingo
These young dingoes know which one is the dominant dog.

The Australian dog
The dingoes of Australia have been so successful at living in the wild that it has only recently been recognized that they were originally domestic dogs taken to Australia by the native Aborigines 4,000 years ago. Dingoes are probably the only purebred descendants left in the world of prehistoric domestic dogs.

Dog aristocrat
The dingo is the most purebred dog in the world, because there are no other wild dogs to breed with.

Mother and babies
Like all dogs, the dingo is descended from the wolf; it mates once a year and raises its pups as social hunters.

Dingo's feet are like a wolf's—there is no dew claw on the hind foot

Coat is a tawny-yellow with pale underparts

Tail is long and bushy—sometimes with a white tip

Feet are white in color

Lurcher shows typical dog bone structure

Breeding dogs

Many dog breeds are hundreds of years old, but a new breed can be developed by crossing two or more different breeds. It is also possible to reconstitute (remake) an extinct breed, such as the Irish wolfhound, which died out 100 years ago and was bred as a new line from Great Danes, deerhounds, and mastiffs (pp. 48–49). Before the first dog show in England in 1859, dogs of one breed came in many sizes, shapes, and colors. Today, they all look similar because of showing standards. This can be harmful, because dogs lose their individual characteristics. It can lead to inherited ailments.

"Ye olde mimicke dogge"
In the late 1500s, an imaginary "Mimicke Dogge" was thought to have a shaggy coat and be good at tricks; others thought it had an "ape's wit and a hedgehog's face."

The turned-up corners of the mouth make this lurcher look as if it is smiling

Lurcher

It's raining cats, dogs, and pitchforks
This old English saying, caricatured (above) in the 19th century by George Cruikshank, may be based on ancient Chinese spirits for rain and wind, which were depicted as a cat and a dog.

Secret symbols
American "kings of the road" (tramps) used signs to say if there was a dog or bad dog on a property.

Dog

Bad dog

Wedgwood majolica (glazed earthenware) punch-bowl, decorated with puppet Punch and his clown-dog Toby

38

Bull's eye
Fighting bull terriers (pp. 46–47), like this one in the film *Oliver!*, were developed by crossing bulldogs and terriers in the 1700s. Their erect ears didn't have to be cropped, which was illegal (p. 45).

A fight to the finish
The Staffordshire bull terrier was developed in the English Midlands as a fighting dog, by crossing the bull terrier, bulldog, and Old English terrier (now extinct).

Small, half-pricked ears

Very muscular body

Staffordshire bull terrier

V-shaped ears, falling forward

Dark, deep-set eyes

The rough and the smooth
First bred in the 1800s by Englishman Jack Russell, these small dogs were produced by several now-extinct breeds, and they varied in appearance. Most Kennel Clubs consider them a type, not a breed, but the Parson Jack Russell is now a breed in Britain, as in the Australian Jack Russell in Australia.

Coat can be long and rough-haired, or short and smooth

Jack Russell terriers

Streamlined body and short-haired coat—built for speed

Thomas Bewick's (p. 43) engraving of a lurcher

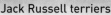

In the lurch
Originally a crossbreed (pp. 60–61) between a greyhound and a terrier, its patience, intelligence, speed, and fighting ability made the lurcher perfect for a poacher (pp. 40–41). A "type" of dog, it may soon be a recognized breed, as many owners would like to enter their dogs in the show ring.

Head over heels
It's hard to say what breed this little dog is, but he has amusing antics.

Hunting dogs

Dogs were used in hunting wild animals for centuries. In medieval times, kings and feudal lords of Europe hunted from horseback with dogs—necessary training for tournaments of chivalry and for warfare. The laws of hunting were very complicated, and certain animals were preserved for the nobility to hunt. Special breeds of scent and sight hound (pp. 14–17) were used during these hunts. The most valuable dogs were buckhounds.

Hunting in India
The Mogull emperors of India also had rituals of hunting. Akbar (1542–1605) is shown here hunting Indian antelope with Saluki-type hounds.

Medieval hunting dogs
Medieval huntsmen usually had 12 running hounds and a lyme-hound (scent hound), which frightened game out of its hiding place, such as in this picture from *Benninck's Book of Hours*.

Come blow the horn
Blowing the horn with a series of long and short notes was a very important part of the rituals of medieval hunting.

The Savernake Horn, made of ivory in 12th-century England

The thrill of the chase
A horserider and hunting dogs chase a stag along this 1845 French watch chain.

Gamekeeper and his dogs
Many traditions of hunting and shooting remain unchanged since medieval times, such as the gamekeeper's job of protecting game from poachers.

Benin piece
The Benin bronzes from Nigeria are famous for their artistic value. This 16th-century plaque is of a Portuguese soldier with his hunting dog.

Running with the pack
The bold, strong, intelligent beagles, such as in this late-19th-century painting by Alfred Duke, may have an ancient origin; the Norman French used them to pursue hares and they were small enough to be carried in hunters' pockets.

Swimming dog
Most dogs enjoy swimming, but retrievers are specially bred to bring back birds and other animals that have been shot and have fallen into the water. These dogs are trained to respond quickly to commands. They have "a soft mouth," which means they can carry a dead bird without biting into it. Their fur has a very thick, water-resistant undercoat.

Diana the huntress
This painting in enamel on a metal plaque from Limoges shows hunting hounds in France in the mid-16th century, with Diana, the Roman goddess of the hunt. Legends says she shunned male society and was attended by nymphs. In classical art, she was often shown in a chariot drawn by two white stags.

All dogs swim by paddling with their front legs, just like children do when they are learning to swim by "doggy-paddling."

Herding dogs

Lassie
The collie got a new name from the *Lassie* films.

The use of dogs to protect and herd livestock dates from 1000 BCE, when farmers began to breed large numbers of animals. In the first century, Roman writer Columella noted that shepherds preferred white sheepdogs so they would not mistake them for a wolf killing their animals. Even today, although the wolf is nearly extinct, most herding dogs are light-colored with white in their coats.

Old dog's tail
Old English sheepdogs are seldom born without tails—most are docked (p. 45) for showing, although a heavy sheepdog with no tail is not much use since it cannot run fast. It is called "Old," but this breed is probably not of ancient origin.

Collie
This traditional sheepdog of the Scottish lowlands is probably so-called from a "colley" (local black sheep). Today, it is a popular show breed and companion.

Straight, muscular forelegs and powerful, sinewy hindlegs enabled the collie to cover great distances while herding sheep

Long-haired, thick coat is usually pale with dark head hair

Belgian shepherd
There were no wolves left in Belgium when their shepherd dogs were first developed in the 1880s, and so they, and the modern German shepherd dog, are not light-colored.

Border collie
Originally from the border of England and Scotland, it is one of the world's finest sheepdogs.

Blue heeler
Now called the Australian cattle dog, this breed of strong working dog, developed by cattlemen in the 1830s, rounds up cattle by nipping at their heels.

A shepherd and his dog

This Romanian shepherd and his dog are prepared for winter. These traditional sheepdog breeds are heavily built, have thick coats, and are good guardians of the flock.

Thomas Bewick engraving

A dog teases a bull in this engraving.

Semierect ears with forward pointing tips

Small but beautiful

All the domestic animals on the Shetland Isles tend to be very small. Small animals thrive best in the tough conditions of cold, wind, and scarce food. The Shetland sheepdog, or sheltie, is a successful product of breeding for small size, and was the traditional herding dog of the Shetland Isles.

The sheltie's good sense of smell can seek out a lamb buried in the snow

Helper dogs

Running to catch a thief

Dogs have been indispensable helpers throughout history. They have been used to herd other animals, for companionship, and as guardians of homes and businesses—although to shut a dog in an enclosed space on its own goes against all the social behavioral patterns of the dog and is cruel. Police dogs are seldom alone and normally live balanced lives. Certain breeds are more innately aggressive than others, but nearly all dogs have to be trained to be aggressive to strangers and not to their handlers. Today, dogs also help the sick, the disabled, and the lonely.

Dogs of war
Dog loyalty to people means they can be trained for dangerous missions.

Strong teeth and a sturdy jaw—with the lower jaw projecting above the upper—help the boxer to keep strangers at bay

Boxers have great strength and energy— the powerful forequarters are inherited from the bulldog

Thick black-and-tan coat is long and wavy, and provides perfect protection against the intense cold of the Swiss mountains

Bernese mountain dog
The dogs known as Swiss mountain dogs until the 1900s today have four breeds: Bernese (p. 57), Appenzell, Entelbuch, and Greater Swiss.

Saint Bernard to the rescue

Rescue dogs
Dogs bred at the monastery of Great Saint Bernard Pass in Switzerland were trained to rescue mountaineers.

Three-headed dog
In ancient mythology, Cerberus stood at the gates of hell to prevent the living from entering and the dead from leaving.

Space dogs
The first dog sent into space was the Russian dog Laika in 1957. Such space missions contributed to human knowledge, but must have been terrifying for the dogs.

БЕЛКА и СТРЕЛКА

Seeing-eye dogs

Dogs can be trained to be "the eyes" of the blind, to help the deaf and disabled, and to provide companionship to the old and sick.

German shepherd dogs have plenty of room in their straight, wolflike jaws for strong, healthy teeth

Cropping dogs' ears to make them erect is illegal in some countries, but not all. It makes them look fiercer

Cutting off the tail (docking) prevents the dog from expressing its natural behavior

This Dobermann is warning an intruder to stay back

The fierce Dobermann

The Dobermann, developed in Germany in the late 19th century, is a born guard dog, bred to be aggressive. But it can also be an affectionate companion.

Good companions

Boxer and German shepherd dogs (p. 11) are guard dogs, first bred in Germany. The boxer is of mastiff origin (pp. 34–35), crossed with the bulldog (p. 54). The German shepherd dog is a droving, or herding, dog. Dogs of both breeds are also affectionate and loyal companions for people if reared correctly, but they need lots of space and exercise.

Powerful hindquarters make the German shepherd dog a good jumper, and able to cover great distances without getting tired

Brave guard

As long as this dog spends most time with a person, it will be content and can be trained to guard people and land.

Sport dogs

Going to the dogs
Greyhounds and whippets are the dog-racing choice. Here, a greyhound advertises Camembert cheese.

Dogs have been used in many cruel sports in the past. In Roman times, baiting (setting dogs against a confined animal) was fashionable and continued until the late 1800s. Today, dog fighting and baiting are illegal in the US. Dogs like to compete with each other and there are sports that are not cruel. Sight hounds (pp. 14–15) have been developed for coursing (chasing after) fast-running prey, and were often used in falconry. In northern Africa and Asia, Saluki and Afghan hounds (p. 48) were bred for chasing gazelles. Today, in greyhound racing, dogs are bred for speed, and run after a mechanical "hare."

"The dog fight"
The spectators in this painting are urging on their dogs to fight. Today, this cruel sport is illegal in many countries.

Keen sight of the borzoi (p. 15) will help it to win a race—or, as in former times, to hunt well

Muzzled
Dogs get excited when they are racing, so usually wear muzzles to stop them from biting other dogs in a race.

Long, muscular lower legs

Borzoi

Deep chest and freely swinging shoulders enable the dog to take long strides

Feathered tail is long, set low, and gently curved

Muscular legs make the Saluki a powerful runner

The royal Saluki

One of the oldest breeds of sight hound (pp. 14–15), found in tomb paintings of ancient Egyptian pharaohs, they have long been bred by Arabs for chasing gazelle and killing large birds.

Off to the races

Dogs have been used to draw sleds (pp. 56–57) for hundreds of years. Today, snowmobiles have replaced them, but the sport of sled-racing with huskies has become very popular in Alaska.

Tintin and Snowy

These popular cartoon characters race over the snow with their trusty team of huskies.

Dense, curly ruff on neck

Long, wavy, silky hair is usually white with attractive dark markings

Ankle joint, or hock, is high up, which makes the leg very long and powerful

The hare and the dog

The use of greyhounds for hare-coursing—pursuing game with dogs that follow by sight, not scent—is probably one of the most ancient of all sports.

Bounder

Once called Russian wolfhounds because the aristocracy used them for hunting and chasing wolves, the borzoi may have been developed from long-legged sight hounds crossed with long-haired, collie-type dogs. They were bred to look regal for emperors.

Hounds

When dogs were separated into groups, hounds were one of the most distinctive. At a later stage, hounds were split into lightly built, very fast sight hounds (pp. 14–15) used in the hunt to chase prey, and heavily built scent hounds (pp. 16–17) used to sniff out prey. Hounds vary in size more than any other dog group. The Irish wolfhound is the heaviest dog; the dachshund, one of the smallest. Many breeds are still used for hunting; others are house dogs and companions. The lifespan of small hounds is about 15 years, but it is half this for large hounds.

Elegant borzoi
The borzoi (p. 15) is the most aristocratic-looking of all hounds.

Welsh legend
The town of Beddgelert in Wales is named after the deerhound Gelert, killed by Prince Llewellyn after he thought the dog had killed his child. But then he found the baby safe, and nearby a dead wolf, killed by his faithful dog.

Wrinkled brow and face

Long, silky ears

"Dewlap" or loose folds of skin hanging beneath the throat

Short hair on face and along the back

Afghan hound
This ancient breed of long-haired greyhound originated in Afghanistan, where the royal family used it for hunting gazelle. When it was first shown in Britain, its long, silky coat caused a sensation. It is a popular show dog but retains its hunting and racing instincts.

Very long, silky hair

Tallyho
The foxhound has changed little since medieval times. It does not make a good house pet because it has been bred only for hunting and living in a pack.

A dignified dog
Today, the bloodhound's role is as a guard dog, but its reputation as a relentless tracker is legendary. Breeding for show standards has led to extreme skin folds around its head, resulting in health problems.

Hound of the Baskervilles

Shown above is a still from one of the films of British writer Sir Arthur Conan Doyle's most famous Sherlock Holmes story.

Tail is carried erect, not curled forward

The great dog of Ireland

The hound breed used in Ireland since medieval times for hunting wolves looked like a rough-haired greyhound. It probably died out in the 1800s—more than 100 years after the last wolf. A British army officer re-created the breed in the late 1800s, and it is the tallest dog in the world, with a shoulder height of 3 ft (94 cm).

Hunting hare

The beagle was originally bred to track hares in Britain and France, but is now popular in North America for hunting rabbits. Because it is small with a uniform weight and tolerates living in large numbers, it is the breed most used in laboratory research.

Hunting tapestry

This detail, from one of four Flemish tapestries woven in the early 1400s, shows a medieval hunting scene with richly dressed ladies and noblemen, their hounds, and boar prey.

"Sausage" dog

Dachshund means "badger-dog" in German, since they were originally used to dig out badgers from their dens. "Hund" was translated as "hound," and so the dogs were classed in that group. The miniature dachshund is a popular house pet.

Straight, strong forelegs and long, muscular hindlegs enabled the Irish wolfhound to chase prey over great distances

The dachshund can have three varieties of coat—short-haired, long-haired, or, as here, wire-haired

Sporting

Ready, aim, fire
The hunter's dog must not be afraid of the noise of a gun.

Spaniels, setters, pointers, and retrievers are all "sporting dogs" (North America), or "gun dogs" (Britain). They are not usually aggressive, and today they are mostly used for hunting game birds. These dogs are trained to "point" and "set" (pp. 16–17)—scent the air for birds, then crouch still and silent to alert the hunters. They must have soft mouths to retrieve prey and not damage it (pp. 40–41). Sporting dogs respond well to training, and so are also bred as house dogs and companions.

English setter holds a stick in its mouth, in the same way as it would a bird

An object for training a sporting dog for holding prey in its mouth

English setter's thick coat enables it to be used for hunting in winter and to endure the cold weather

At the end of the day
Along with their hunting dogs (pp. 40–41) , these hunters, wearing hacking jackets and riding breeches, are resting after a hunt.

Bringing home a bird
The retriever is trained to retrieve game after it has been shot.

Setters and pointers often hold up one front foot as they "freeze" into position before the shoot

Red-haired beauty
The Irish, or red, setter has a silky coat and gentle nature, but is high-strung and headstrong—no good for a sporting dog.

A real charmer
The cocker spaniel got its name because it flushes out woodcock birds.

Muscular, strong-boned legs helped the cocker to be an excellent bird dog

A damp day for duck hunting
Spaniels, bred for centuries as water dogs, are the traditional companions of the bird hunter. In this painting are a Chesapeake retriever, curly coated retriever, and Irish water spaniel.

Getting the point
Pointers are trained to "point" (p. 17) at game with their noses.

Dog decoration made of Italian glass, c. 1800

Tail is called "feathered" when it looks like the feathers of a bird

Good shot
This 18th-century tile from France shows a hunter and his sporting dogs chasing the prey, which is probably a rabbit.

Setting up the game
The English setter is one of the oldest and most beautiful breed of sporting dog. Originally, the setter was a spaniel, trained to "set" the game—to put the birds up to be killed. In the Middle Ages, birds were caught in nets.

Special long lead allows sporting dogs to escape their leash quickly

Terriers

Terriers are "earth dogs"—*terra* means "the earth" in Latin. They are great diggers and will happily go down holes after badgers, foxes, rabbits, or rats. Terriers have an ancient history in Britain as small sporting and hunting dogs. Different types of terrier have been bred in many regions of Britain, but a few other countries have also developed new breeds, such as the Australian terrier.

Scottie dog
The modern Scottish terrier, descended from working terriers that were bred for centuries in the Scottish Highlands, were not black until the 1900s.

The tip of the Airedale's small, V-shaped ear falls forward to the top of its eye

Strong teeth and vicelike jaws hold prey tightly

Coat is stiff, wiry, and lies close to the body, thereby requiring careful grooming (pp. 62–63)

Long, strong jaws help the Australian terrier catch rabbits, rats, and even snakes

A shaggy dog story
Early British immigrants to Australia took their dogs. By the early 1900s, the Australian terrier had been developed from a mix of Cairn, Dandie Dinmont, Irish, Scottish, and Yorkshire terriers.

A Roman dog
This copper alloy figure (made between the first and fourth centuries) looks like the old Aberdeen breed.

The terrier has a playful nature

The ears of the low-slung Norfolk terrier are slightly rounded at the tip and drop forward close to its cheek

The giant Airedale terrier

The largest of all terriers was developed in the mid-1800s by crossbreeding (pp. 60–61) the black-and-tan terrier with the otterhound to increase its size and strength.

Tail is set high up and carried erect, not curved forward over its back

Legendary

When "Greyfriars" died in Edinburgh, Scotland, his Skye-type terrier, Bobby, refused to leave his grave until he died 10 years later. Or so the story goes.

Fox terrier

In the late 1800s, this was England's most popular breed; today, it is the smaller Jack Russell. Fox terriers can be wire- or smooth-haired.

With excellent balance, a wire-haired fox terrier is ready for action

Decorated dog

Dogs are popular mascots with army regiments, like this brave war hero, "Drummer," mascot of the Northumberland Fusiliers.

Long ears and curly coat make it look like a lamb

Like a lamb

All kinds of breeds contributed to the development of the Bedlington terrier, once known as the Rothbury terrier.

Dandified dog

Dogs have long been used in advertising.

Norfolk terrier

This new breed, descended from terriers bred in East Anglia, England, is a sporting dog with short legs and a wiry coat. Originally the drop-eared Norwich variety, it was given the name of Norfolk in 1965.

Terriers dig with both front legs and hindlegs

Utility dogs

The word "utility" means usefulness. Most dogs are useful to humans, and so this collection includes dogs that haven't been categorized under one of the other five groups (pp. 48–53, 56–59). "Special dogs" might be a more apt term to use, since this group includes interesting, often unusual dogs. For some, their history goes back many centuries, and most of this group have been bred for a particular purpose—for instance, the bulldog for bullbaiting, and the poodle for hunting water fowl. But today, these dogs live as companions and show dogs. This group also includes national dogs from various countries.

American
The Boston terrier is one of the few breeds to have been developed in the US.

Useful helpers
A 17th-century Portuguese merchant is shown with his servants—and faithful dog.

The back has retained the powerful muscles of the old-fashioned bulldog

Bat-eared bulldog
French bulldogs were once used for baiting donkeys (p. 46). Today, they are smaller and more peaceful, but are still tough and make good guard dogs.

Legs are set wide apart, allowing the dog to stand its ground

French bulldog

The tongue of the chow chow is always blue-black, an unusual characteristic inherited from the dog's Chinese ancestors

Chinese chow
The chow chow breed is now 200 years old, developed from two dogs of pariah origin (p. 36) that were introduced into England from Canton, southeast China, in the 1780s.

Very thick fur and curled tails are typical of spitz dogs, like the chow chow, for adapting to subarctic temperatures

The best of British
The bulldog is a British national symbol, portraying strength and stubbornness. It was developed for bullbaiting—setting dogs to attack bulls for public sport—and dates back to at least the 16th century.

Circus tricks
The poodle is easily trained and so was commonly used as a circus dog, as depicted in this c. 1890 Austrian gold brooch.

Muzzle is adorned by a massive mustache

The strongest schnauzer, the giant schnauzer stands 2 ft (65 cm) at the shoulder

Schnauzers
So-called from *Schnauze*, meaning muzzle in German, and bred for herding sheep in southern Germany, these energetic dogs make good family pets. In North America, the giant and standard schnauzer are classified as "working dogs" (pp. 56–57); the miniature, "terriers" (pp. 52–53).

The elegant "coach dog"
In England and France in the 1800s, it was fashionable to have a "coach dog" to accompany the carriages of aristocrats.

The Dalmatian's coat is always pure white with distinctive black or brown (liver) spots

Spotted dog
There are several legends about the origin of the Dalmatian, including that they came from India with the Roma to Dalmatia, Croatia. Dalmatians were first taken to England in the 18th century, where these aristocratic-looking dogs were used as coach dogs (see above). The Dalmatian is unique in that it excretes urea, not uric acid, in its urine, which means its urine does not kill lawn grass—a gardener's best friend.

Legs are long and built for speed and endurance

Pretty as a picture
Poodles were first bred as sporting dogs (pp. 50–51), probably in Germany, but because of their intelligence and good looks they soon became house dogs. This painting shows a 1700s form of the pet.

Working dogs

Superior swimmer
The huge Newfoundland may come from Pyrenean mountain rescue dogs taken to Newfoundland, Canada, by Spanish fishermen.

About 12,000 years ago, tamed wolves were bred to be the first domestic dogs (pp. 34–35) as companions to human hunters. Since then, dogs have worked with people. Dogs were the only domesticated animal of Native Americans, who used them to draw a travois (sled) and in bison hunts. In Europe, horses and oxen, rather than dogs, were used for pulling carts, although Inuit dogs and huskies were part of polar explorations. For dog shows, herding dogs (pp. 42–43) and helper dogs (pp. 44–45) fall in the "working dogs" category.

Royal corgi
These short-legged cattle dogs are favorites of British royalty.

Color of a husky's eyes can be brown or blue—or even one of each

Agile Aussie
Australian kelpies round up sheep that have strayed from the main flock, running along sheep's backs to reach the head of the flock. They can travel 40 miles (64 km) in a day.

Siberian husky

Dogs lose heat through their tongues, which is why they pant to cool down—even in the Arctic

Thick ruff of fur around nec, and stocky shape keep as much warmth inside the husky's body as possible

Swiss blanket
The Bernese mountain dog, a typical helper dog (pp. 44–45), is one of many mastiff-type dogs used in Europe and Asia since the Roman period for guarding and protecting mountain travelers. By sleeping beside the traveler, its very thick fur would keep both warm, and it could find the way with its nose even through thick snow.

Special delivery
In Switzerland and other mountainous countries, mastiff-type dogs were best for pulling milk carts steadily along narrow paths. From earliest times (pp. 34–35), its natural aggression made the mastiff an excellent guard dog.

In the great far north

"Eskimo" means "snow." The name is used when describing the dogs of the native, Arctic-dwelling North Americans.

The Great Dane, like all mastiffs, has a very deep and powerful chest

When is a Dane not a Dane?

The Great Dane was developed in Germany for guarding castles.

The working dog's harness is designed to give it the greatest pulling power

The tail trails when the dog is working or at rest, but curves over its back when running

Harnessing a husky

The Siberian husky and Alaskan malamute are the only pure breeds of husky. But the name is used in North America for all dogs of the spitz type, used for drawing sleds and hunting Arctic animals. Arctic peoples could not have survived without working huskies and Eskimo dogs (pp. 46–47).

Heraldic dogs

This husky is part of the coat of arms for Canada's Yukon Territory.

Toy dogs

This category includes all the smallest show breeds, mostly with a height of less than 12 in (30 cm). Remarkably, every single toy dog is descended from the wolf—even the tiniest has inherited the same characteristics as its wild ancestor, and will therefore try its best to behave like a wolf. It will gnaw at bones, guard its territory, and show its feelings with its posture and tail. The Romans were probably the first to breed miniature dogs. Other tiny dogs have been bred since ancient times in Tibet, China, and Japan, while in Europe, toy spaniels were the favorite companions of the aristocracy throughout the Middle Ages.

Dismal Desmond—
a popular stuffed toy
from 1930s England

V-shaped,
small ears
set high

Fine, long, silky-
textured coat

Dog's dinner
This 19th-century French painting, *Caninemania*, shows the family pet treated as a dinner guest. The lady's friend has been relegated to a corner—out of the picture.

Large, broad head
with very flat profile
and a snub nose

Toy terrier terror
The Australian silky terrier can kill a rat, rabbit, or even snake in seconds. It looks like a Yorkshire terrier, but apparently originated by crossbreeding in Australia.

Chinese lion dog
Another name for the Pekingese is the "Lion Dog of Peking." Legend says that they were first bred to represent the lion spirit of Buddha. Today, they look more like a cuddly toy than a lion.

A Pekingese walks with
a rolling gait to distribute
its weight evenly

Pekingese pair
Miniature dogs have been in China for at least 2,500 years, but the Pekingese breed is unlikely to be ancient. It was taken to England after the sacking of the Summer Palace in Peking (now Beijing) in 1860.

A popular pinscher

The miniature pinscher is an older breed than the Dobermann pinscher, and show standards have meant the tail is docked (p. 45), preventing the dog from expressing its emotions and upsetting its balance when running.

Pomeranian

In the 18th century, the Pomeranian breed was much larger than it is today. It is a miniature spitz and has the stocky body, pricked ears, ruff of fur, and curled tail that is typical of this group of northern dogs (p. 54).

Head is rounded with a turned-up nose

Royal favorite

Probably originating in China or Japan, this good-natured dog was named because of English king Charles II's fondness for it.

The miniature pinscher has the strong legs of a much larger dog

King Charles spaniel

The tail of the Bichon is always curled over its back

Bichon frise

Recently, the Bichon Frise ("curly lap dog") has become more popular, especially in the US. It is a Franco-Belgian breed, like a small poodle, and is a lively little dog.

The white coat has a very soft wooly underfur and an upper layer of loosely curled, silky hairs

Crossbred dogs

The development of breeds for different purposes has been a long process, stretching more than 5,000 years. However, most dogs are still mongrels, or "crossbred" dogs, which have interbred with each other; purebred dogs (pp. 48–59) of the same breed have been selectively bred by humans. All 400 breeds of dog can interbreed because they are all descended from the wolf (pp. 8–9)—they are the same species, meaning that many unlikely crosses have occurred. It is often claimed that crossbred dogs are more intelligent than purebreds, but it is more likely their behavior shows variation because they combine different breeds' characteristics.

Sitting dog
This mutt is eagerly waiting for its reward.

Tail arched upward helps dog retain balance

Giant leap for dogkind
These pictures show how a crossbred dog jumps over an obstacle. The tail is important for keeping balance.

Strong, muscular legs help this dog to jump high off the ground at the beginning of its leap

Correct stance for takeoff

Good dog!
Training a dog to establish good behavior patterns can be a long and arduous process.

"His master's voice"
This painting was bought by a gramophone company. The dog was a crossbred, with a lot of bull terrier. The picture and slogan were trademarked in 1910, and are still the sign of a famous record company.

On the doghouse
The cartoon dog Snoopy is mainly a beagle with a bit of something else. Like most dogs, he likes to sleep and dream, especially on top of his doghouse.

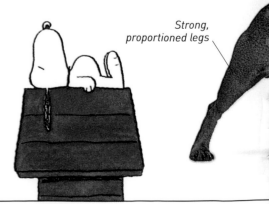

Strong, proportioned legs

Waiting, waiting

A dog's wagging tail is seen as a friendly gesture toward others. This small figure of a pet dog, made of terra-cotta in 500 BCE, was found in Boeotia in central Greece.

Dogs' best friend

This poignant painting, *L'Ami des Bêtes*, shows an old tramp sharing his little food with his only friends—a large group of mongrels.

Keeping its cool

This crossbred puppy (pp. 20–21) is licking its nose to help keep cool.

Bright, alert eyes

Medium-length coat, neither too short, nor too long

Tail arches over back when dog touches down

Well-defined body outline

Front legs are straight and feet firmly on the ground when jump is completed

Well-shaped nose

Pert, expressive ears

A motley crew

These crossbred dogs have no extremes of form or function. Crossbreeds are often tougher, better-tempered, less disease-prone, and more adaptable than purebreds.

Dog care

Dog ownership lasts for the animal's life—up to 17 years. For the first year, training a puppy is like bringing up a child, although a dog can be house-trained faster than a child. The dog's every need must be attended to, and it must be taught its place within the family. A dog should never be left on its own for more than a few hours. It needs clean drinking water, regular meals at set times, and hard biscuits or bones to keep its teeth clean. It should be treated for parasites and inoculated against any diseases.

Bathtime for Bonzo
This little girl is intent on keeping her pet clean.

1. Ready and waiting for a grooming session

2. A partially clipped poodle

3. Fine-tuning underneath

Good grooming
The poodle is a water dog (p. 55), and its coat has to be clipped to stop it from matting and for the dog's comfort.

4. Bathtime

5. Perfecting the tail

6. The end result

Bowl of water at all times

Dish of dry, crunchy dog food

Assortment of dog biscuits

And so to bed
In the same way that a wild wolf has its own den, every domestic dog needs its own bed. This can be a basket, a bean bag, or a chair the dog has made its own.

Brush and comb

Favorite toys

Doggy chew

Leash

Collar

Essential aids for looking after a dog

Dense coat of a poodle requires special grooming

Cleaning the teeth

Clipping the claws

Trimming hair between the claws

Stray dogs
For a dog, to be lost or abandoned by its owner is very frightening. If it is taken to a home for stray dogs, it will be anxious and confused. If a dog can no longer be kept, and no new home is available, then the kindest thing is to have a vet put the dog to sleep.

The winner is...
Dog shows have been held for 100 years. The shows maintain breed standards and allow breeders to discuss achievements and problems of the breed. However, show standards for breeds are not always in the best interest of the dogs. Docking (p. 45), for instance, is not a beneficial practice.

NAME............ TEL........
ADDRESS
....

Identification
Every dog must carry its owner's name and address on its collar, as a code in a tattoo, or by a tiny coded pellet under the skin.

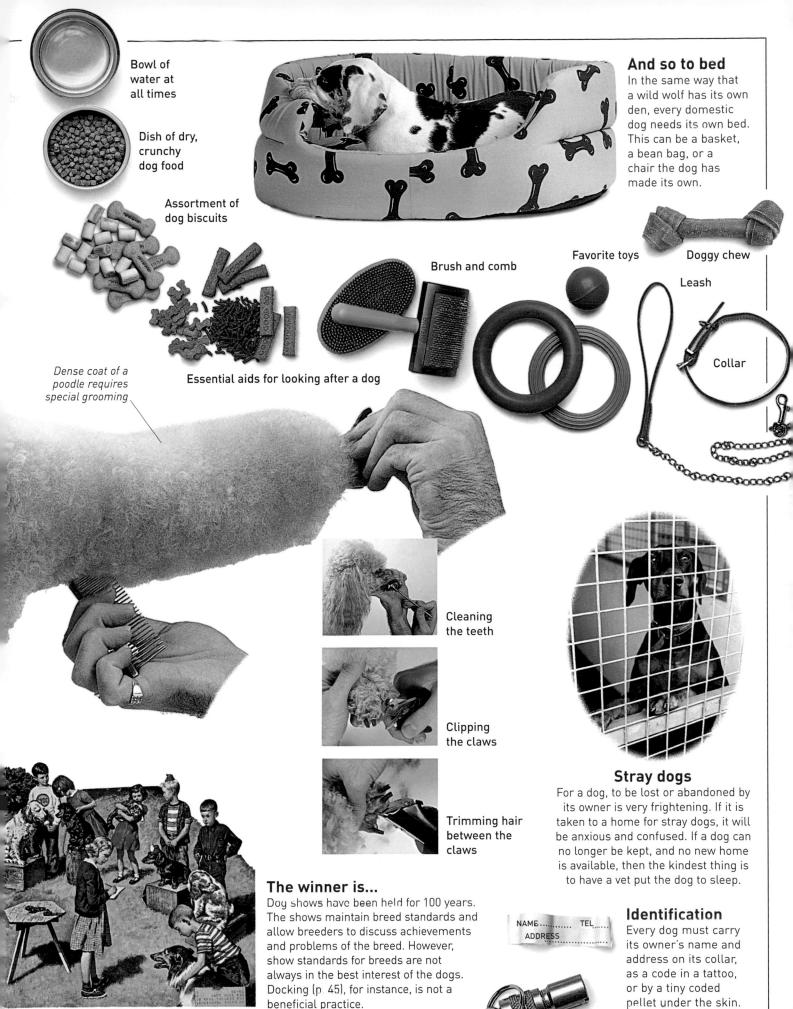

Did you know?

AMAZING FACTS

Dogs can smell and hear better than they can see. Dogs see things first by movement, second by brightness, and third by shape.

Rhodesian ridgebacks have a visible ridge of forward-growing hairs running along their backs.

A dog's sense of smell is 1,000 times better than ours. "Scent" dogs can identify several different scents at the same time. Dogs have 20–25 times more smell-receptor cells than people do.

A mother suckling her young

Hair from some dogs, such as the Samoyed, can be spun into thread and woven into clothes.

Dogs can hear high-pitched sounds that humans are not aware of, can hear from a great distance, and can figure out the direction of a faint sound.

The basenji, an African wolf dog, is the only dog breed not able to bark.

Basenji

Dogs eat quickly and can regurgitate food easily. This is useful for wolves, who travel back to their dens to regurgitate food for pups. It also helps dogs get rid of bad food.

Long-faced dogs have eyes on the sides of their heads, and so have a wide field of vision. Short-faced dogs have forward-facing eyes, which makes them good at judging distance.

Big dogs tend to have larger litters than small dogs, but small dogs usually live longer.

Bulldogs were originally bred to bait and fight bulls and bears.

Dogs have about 10 vocal sounds; cats about 20. Dogs communicate a lot by body language—puppies know signals before words.

Almost one in three families in France and the US own a dog. In Germany and Switzerland, there is only one dog for every 10 households.

On average, there are 320 bones in a dog's skeleton, depending on the length of its tail.

A dog was the first animal to go into space. In 1957, Russian scientists sent Laika in a satellite.

The greyhound is one of the oldest breed of dog.

A Newfoundland dog swimming

Newfoundland dogs are good swimmers. Like many breeds, they have webbing between their toes, helping them paddle through water.

A puppy is deaf for three weeks, until its ear canals open up.

Most puppies have 28 temporary teeth, which they begin to lose at about 12 weeks. They have usually grown their 42 permanent teeth by the time they are six months old.

Unlike cats, dogs cannot retract (pull in) their claws.

Bloodhounds have an amazing sense of smell. They can follow scent trails that are four days old.

Bloodhound

QUESTIONS AND ANSWERS

A dog searching a car for drugs

Record Breakers

THE OLDEST DOG
An Australian cattle dog named Bluey lived to be 29 years and five months old.

THE HEAVIEST AND LONGEST DOG
An Old English mastiff named Zorba holds the record as the heaviest and longest dog. In 1989, it weighed 343 lb (155 kg) and was 8 ft 3 in (2.5 m) long.

THE TALLEST AND SMALLEST BREEDS
The smallest dog breed is the chihuahua. Dogs from several breeds can be 36 in (90 cm) at the shoulder, and they are classed as the tallest breeds—the Great Dane, Irish wolfhound, Saint Bernard, English mastiff, borzoi, and Anatolian karabash.

Great Dane

Q Why do the police use dogs?

A Because of the dogs' excellent sense of smell. "Sniffer" dogs help police track down escaped prisoners and find illegal drugs.

Q Why do dogs chase their tails?

A A puppy instinctively chases its tail, perhaps because it resembles moving prey. If an adult dog chases its tail, it either needs exercise or has a medical problem.

Q Which dogs are the smartest?

A Most sheepdog and gun dog breeds are intelligent and easy to train. Some smaller breeds are very good at performing tricks.

Q How should you approach a strange dog?

A To get close to an unfamiliar dog, kneel down and let it sniff the back of your hand. Do not make sudden movements or stare into its eyes—that might feel like a threat. Do not run, as that could encourage it to chase you.

Q Why do dogs pant?

A Unlike people, dogs cannot cool themselves by perspiring. They have sweat glands only in their feet. But panting helps a dog stay cool—saliva evaporating from the tongue and mouth helps reduce its body heat.

Q Why do dogs eat grass?

A Dogs often eat grass when they are sick. It makes them throw up and then they feel better.

Border collies often herd sheep

Q Can dogs see in color?

A A dog's color vision is limited to gray and blue. The colors green, red, yellow, and orange look the same.

Q Why do dogs' eyes glow in the dark?

A A layer of cells, called the "tapetum lucidum", at the back of each eye of a dog reflects light, making it possible for it to see in dim light. When a bright light strikes a dog's eyes, it is reflected, making the eyes appear to glow.

Q What is a dorgi?

A When a dachshund and a corgi mate, their offspring are called dorgis.

Identifying dogs

Dogs come in different sizes. The American Kennel Club recognizes 178 breeds, and divides them into seven groups, according to the dog's role.

HEAD SHAPES

Long-headed dogs have a long, often tapering nose. Round-headed breeds have a short nose. Square-headed dogs have a step between the muzzle and the forehead. It is known as the "stop."

A beagle has a square muzzle

A pug has a very flat face

The borzoi has long, powerful jaws

Square head

Rounded head

Long head

COAT TYPES

Short-haired dogs have a smooth coat. Most long-haired breeds have a thick undercoat with a longer coat on top. Wire-haired dogs have a short undercoat with longer, wiry hairs on top. A few breeds have a corded, feltlike coat.

Long-haired Old English sheepdog

Short-haired Entelbuch mountain dog

Wire-haired schnauzer

Hungarian puli

Greyhounds have excellent sight

Racing greyhounds wear coats with numbers

Hounds

People have long bred dogs to catch other animals. Some very fast hounds are "sight" hounds, which means that they chase things they can see. Other hounds have great stamina and pursue by scent.

Dalmatian puppies are colored pure white when they are born; their spots develop as they grow

Utility dogs

This group contains many different dogs, bred for specific functions not categorized as working or sporting. The Dalmatian was a carriage dog—it trotted alongside a carriage to put off potential attackers.

The Jack Russell terrier's coat is mainly white

Terriers

Terriers are alert, bold, and fearless. Most were originally kept as rat catchers on farms. They love digging, and some were used to flush out foxes or to hunt badgers and otters.

Pastoral dogs

Many dogs in this group still herd sheep and cattle today. They are active and intelligent. Most have a double coat, protecting them in rough weather.

Chihuahua

Gun dogs

These friendly and intelligent dogs require lots of exercise. The group includes pointers, spaniels, setters, and retrievers, like this Labrador retriever. Many are good at flushing out and retrieving birds for hunters—some at retrieving waterbirds.

Toy dogs

Known as companion dogs, breeds in this group are friendly, intelligent, love attention, and are mostly small in size.

Working dogs

This group includes guard dogs, such as the mastiff and Dobermann, dogs to pull sleds or carts, like the Siberian husky and Bernese mountain dog, dogs for helping fishermen, such as the Newfoundland, and dogs for search and rescue, such as the Saint Bernard.

Find out more

One of the best ways of finding out more about dogs is to spend time with them. You could walk a neighbor's dog or spend time with friends who have a dog. You could go along to a dog show and watch the competitions and training displays. Or you might consider volunteering to help at a shelter or at the ASPCA.

Tell your puppy immediately if it has done something wrong

Dog training
The Canine Good Citizen Program (CGC) is a national certification program to reward dogs that have demonstrated good manners. CGC is a two-part program to develop responsible pet owners.

A dog must learn to sit obediently at its owner's heels

A pet puppy
If you get a puppy, spend time with it. Dogs relate best to people they've known when they were puppies. Puppies need to be told how to behave, but they also need support, affection, and praise.

Crufts
The largest dog show in the world, with around 150,000 visitors, Crufts is held every March in the UK. There are promotional stands, competitions, and displays. More than 26,000 pedigree dogs compete for the coveted award of "Best in Show."

Crufts
BEST IN SHOW
Pedigree

Crufts
RESERVE BEST IN S

Help dogs in trouble

Help the Humane Society or the American Society for the Prevention of Cruelty to Animals (ASPCA), by giving time or money. Both rescue abandoned and mistreated animals.

An rescue worker comforts a scared dog

The assistance dog provides warmth and affection as well as practical help

Helpful dogs

Well-trained dogs can be a huge help to physically disabled people. The dogs open doors, pick up items, turn lights on and off, go for help, and provide constant companionship. Find out more about charities to see how you can help.

PLACES TO VISIT

**WESTMINSTER KENNEL DOG SHOW
NEW YORK, NEW YORK**

• The second longest-running sports event in the US (behind the Kentucky Derby), the show is held each February at Madison Square Garden in New York. It features over 2,500 dogs from 162 breeds competing to be "Best in Show."

**NATIONAL DOG SHOW
PHILADELPHIA, PENNSYLVANIA**

• Over 2,500 dogs compete for Breed, Group, and "Best in Show" honors.

**THE AMERICAN KENNEL CLUB
MUSEUM OF THE DOG
WEST ST. LOUIS COUNTY, MISSOURI**

• The museum houses one of the finest collections of art devoted to the dog.

LEEDS CASTLE, KENT, ENGLAND

• The castle exhibits a collection of dog collars through the ages.

A dog collar from the collection at Leeds Castle

Agile dogs

Dog shows will help you find out more about what dogs can do. Some shows include agility competitions, in which dogs jump fences, weave through poles, cross seesaws, and go through tunnels. Owners run around the course directing their dogs. The winner is the fastest dog with the fewest penalties.

USEFUL WEBSITES

• Full coverage of the Westminster Dog Show:
www.westminsterkennelclub.org
• Find a dog trainer in your area:
iaabc.org/consultants/dog
• Information about dog breeds:
www.yourpurebredpuppy.com/dogbreeds
• Information about the Humane Society or about adopting a pet: **www.hsus.org**
• Learn about the process for adopting a pet from the ASPCA or for advice about how to care for your pet:
www.aspca.org
• Paws with a Cause trains assistance dogs for people with disabilities:
www.pawswithacause.org
• Information about caring for your pet, or about breeds, dog training, and animal shelters:
www.aboutdogsonline.com

Saint Bernard

Glossary

Beagles have drop ears

BAIT An edible item to attract animals.

BAT EARS Erect ears that are wide at the base, round at the tips, and point out.

BITCH An adult female dog.

BREED A group of dogs with particular characteristics. Humans control breeding for specific features, such as head shape. If the breeding is not supervised, characteristics can be lost.

BREEDING The process of producing animals by mating one with another.

BREED STANDARD The official detail of a breed, setting out size, color, etc.

An Italian greyhound with her puppies

BRINDLE A mix of tan and black hair.

BRUSH A term used to describe a bushy tail; also a fox's tail.

CAMOUFLAGE The coloration of an animal that blends in with the surroundings or breaks up its outline with stripes or spots, making it harder to see. Camouflage can be important for animals that hunt and are hunted.

CANID A member of the dog family; from *canis* (Latin for dog).

CANINE Dog or doglike; it is also the large tooth between the incisors and the premolars, used for gripping prey.

CARNIVORE A member of the order Carnivora, containing animals with specialized teeth for biting and shearing flesh. Most carnivores live on meat.

CROP The removal of the top of the ears so that they stand upright and are pointed at the tip. Cropping is illegal in many countries, although it is still legal in the United States.

CROSSBREED An animal whose parents are from different breeds or who are crossbreeds.

DEN The retreat or resting place of a wild animal.

DEW CLAW The claw on the inside of the legs. It is not for any particular purpose.

DEWLAP The loose folds of skin hanging under a dog's throat.

DOCK To remove an animal's tail, or part of it, by cutting.

DOG Specifically an adult male dog, but used in a general way for all dogs.

DOGGY-PADDLING To swim moving your limbs in vertical circles, in the same way a dog swims.

DOMINANT The animal that is stronger and in a more powerful position in a group.

DOUBLE COAT A coat made up of a soft, insulating undercoat, through which longer guard hairs protrude.

DROP EARS Ears that hang down, close to the sides of the head.

ERECT Standing upright.

FAMILY Any of the taxonomic groups into which an order is divided. A family contains one or more genera. Canidae is the name of the dog family.

FERAL DOGS Domestic dogs, returned to the wild.

FORELEGS The two front legs.

GENUS (plural **GENERA**) Any of the taxonomic groups into which a family is divided. A genus contains one or more species.

GROOM To rub down and clean a dog.

GUARD HAIRS The coarse hairs that form the outer coat of some mammals.

GUN DOGS A group of dogs trained to work with a hunter at pointing, flushing out, and retrieving game.

HINDLEGS The back legs of a four-legged animal.

Labs are sporting dogs

HOUNDS A group of hunting dogs, such as fast, lightly built "sight" hounds, and stocky, relentless "scent" hounds.

JAWS The part of the skull that frames the mouth and holds the teeth.

LIGAMENT The tough tissue that connects bones and cartilage and that support muscle.

Three cross-bred dogs, or mongrels

LITTER A group of puppies born at one time to one female.

MONGREL A dog of mixed or unknown breeding. Also known as crossbred dogs or mutts.

MOLT To lose hair so that new growth can take place. Dogs molt their thick, winter coat in the spring.

MUSCLE Tissue that can contract or relax and, as a result, allow movement.

MUZZLE The part of the head that is in front of the eyes.

PACK A group of animals of the same kind that usually live together, may be related, and hunt together.

PEDIGREE The record of a pure-breed dog's ancestors.

PUPPY A dog less than one year old.

PURE-BREED A dog with parents of the same breed. Also, a pedigree dog.

REGURGITATE To throw up food that has been eaten. Wolves do this to feed their young.

RUFF Long, thick hair around the neck.

SADDLE Black markings in the shape and position of the saddle on a horse.

SCAVENGER An animal that feeds on animal remains that it steals or finds.

SCENT HOUND A dog that has been bred to use its excellent sense of smell more than its sight or hearing when pursuing other animals. Scent hounds include bloodhounds, beagles, and foxhounds.

SIGHT HOUND A dog with excellent sight that will chase game while it can see it. Greyhounds and borzoi are sight hounds.

SKELETON The framework of bones that gives shape to an animal, provides anchorage for muscles, protects vital organs, is a source of blood cells, and stores minerals.

SPECIES Any of the taxonomic groups into which a genus is divided. Members of the same species are able to breed with each other.

SPITZ Any of various breeds of dog characterized by a stocky build, a curled tail, a pointed muzzle, and erect ears. The chow chow is a spitz.

STEREOSCOPIC VISION The ability to see a slightly different picture with each eye, and, by putting them together, to judge distances accurately.

SUCKLE To suck milk from the mother. The term also means to give milk to a young animal.

TAPETUM LUCIDUM The cells at the back of a dog's eye that reflect light; these cells make it possible for a dog to see well when there is not a lot of light.

TENDON A band of tough tissue that attaches a muscle to a bone.

TERRIERS A group of active, inquisitive dogs originally trained to hunt animals living underground.

THIRD EYELID A thin fold of skin in the upper and lower eyelids; it can be drawn across the eye to protect the eye from dirt.

TOY DOGS A group of very small dogs popular as pets.

Yorkshire terrier

UNDERCOAT (or **UNDERFUR**) The dense, soft fur beneath the outer, coarser fur in some mammals.

UTILITY DOGS A variety of different dogs that are useful to humans.

WEAN To cause a puppy to replace its mother's milk with other food.

WORKING DOGS A group of dogs that work for people, for instance, by pulling sleds or herding sheep.

Puppies playing

Index

Acknowledgments

Dorling Kindersley would like to thank:
Trevor Smith's Animal World: V. Battarby, R. Hills, E. Mustoe, H. Neave, D. Peach, R. Ramphul, S. Renton, S. Surrell, J. Williamson, and J. Young for lending dogs for photography. The zoos of Augsburg Duisburg and Osnabrück for providing wild dogs for photography. J. Larner for the grooming section. The British Kennel Club and Mrs. R. Wilford for breed information. The Natural History Museum's staff and R. Loverance of the British Museum for their research help. J. Gulliver for her help in the initial stages of the book. C. Carez, B. Crowley, C. Gillard, T. Keenes, and E. Sephton for their editorial/design assistance. J. Parker for the index.

For this edition the publishers would also like to thank: Niki Foreman for text editing and Carron Brown for proofreading.

Illustrations:
E. Sephton, J. Kaiser-Atcherley

The publisher would like to thank the following for their kind permission to reproduce their photographs:
a=above t=top b=bottom c=center l=left r=right

Advertising Archives: 60bl 63bl. **Allsport:** 46cl / Bob Martin: 15cr. **American Museum of Natural /A E Anderson:** 9tl; /Logan: 9ct. **Ancient Art and Architecture Collection:** 49bcl. **Animal Photography/Sally Anne Thompson:** 39tr 45tr 45br 50c. **Ardea London Ltd/Eric Dragesco:** 25tl; /Ian Beames: 35br; /John Daniels 68c 69bl; / Jean-Paul Ferrero: 22t 37cl 56c; /Kenneth W. Fink: 20bl 31br; /M. Krishnan: 36cbl; /S. Meyers: 28tl. **Australian Overseas Information Service London:** 37tr. **Bridgeman Art Library:** 6tl 6–7t 7tr 40cl 41tl 41tr 42tr; Cadogan Gallery London: 18cl; Oldham Art Gallery Lancs: 46tr; Rafael Valls Gallery London: 55bl. **British Museum:** 34tl 34br 35cl 35bl /Museum of Mankind: 26br. **Jean-Loup Charmet:** 19bl 51bl 58cr 61tr. **Bruce Coleman/John M Burnley:** 19tl; /Jessica Ehlers: 36bl; /Jeff Foott: 32cl; /Gullivan & Rogers: 33br;

/F. Jorge: 32tr; /Leonard Lee Rue: 25tc 29tl. **Columbia Pictures Television:** 39tl. **Corbis:** 64–65 (background) /Gallo Images 25crb / Richard Hamilton Smith 67b /Kevin R Morris 67tr /Tom Nebbia 64tr 69c /Rick Price 66–67 (background) /Ariel Skelley 68tr /Greg Smith 65tl /Dale C. Spartas 67cl. **Syvia Cordaiy Photo Library:** 63cbr. **Cyanamid (UK)/Animal Health Div:** 11b. **C. M. Dixon:** 36tl. **DK Images:** Tracy Morgan 64bl 65cr 66clb 66bl 66cbl 67tl 68–69 (background), 70t 70cl 70b 70–71 (background). **EMI Records:** 60cr. **English Heritage/Keith Hobbs:** 52cr. **e.t. Archive:** 48bl **Mary Evans Picture Library:** 10tl 16bl 21c 22cb 44bl 47bl 48tl 48tr 53tc. **Marc Henrie ASC (London):** 42br©. **Hergé:** 47cr. **Michael Holford:** 4br 34bl 38cl 58bl. **Hutchison Library/H. R. Dörig:** 32tl; /R Ian Lloyd: 35tl. **ILN Picture Library:** 53cl 56br. **Image Bank:** 12tl 30tl. **Imperial War Museum:** 44tr. **Kennel Club Picture Library:** 68b. **Dave King:** 10br 13ctl 39 btr 42 bl 45cr 48cl 51tl 52tl 52–53 53c 54tr 54bl 57tl 61bl. **Kobal Collection:** 42tl; / Avco Embassy: 23br; /Twentieth Century Fox: 49tl. **Michael Leach:** 29cb. **Leeds Castle:** 35bc 69cr/. **Macmillan Inc:** 8br. **National Archive of Canada/Karen E Bailey (C–137830):** 57b. **National Portrait Gallery:** 56tr. **Natural History Museum Pubs:** 9br. **Peter Newark's Pictures:** 25c 29cr. **NHPA/Michael Leach:** 36ctl; /Mandal

Raijit: 27bl. **Robert Opie Collection:** 44tl 50tl 54cr 62tl. **Oxford Scientific Films/O. Newman:** 23cr. **Planet Earth Pictures/J. R. Bracegirdle:** 24bc; /JimBrandenburg: 11cr 23bl; /J Scott: 21tl. **Axel Poignant Archive:** 36br. **Retrograph Archive/Martin Breese:** 14tr 20tl 42cl 44br 46tl 50cl 53cr. **Reuters /Andy Muller:** 66cr **RSPCA Photolibrary /Paul Herrmann:** 69tl. **Gary Santry:** 61cr. **Science Photo Library/John Sanford:** 8tl. **South American Pictures/Tony Morrison:** 33bl. **Tate Gallery:** 59tr. **Tring Museum:** 7bl. ©1990 **United Feature Syndicate Inc:** 60br. **F R Valla:** 35cr. **V & A Museum:** 29br 56tl 58tl. **Werner Forman Archive:** 23ct 24tr 41tc 54tl. **Zefa Picture Library:** 47cl. /©**Dr Erik Zimen:** 18ctr 19tr 21cl 23tr.

All other images © Dorling Kindersley

For further information see:
www.dkimages.com